THE
BEST JOKES
ON
EARTH

Mel Foster

CONTENTS

ACKNOWLEDGMENTS

The list of people who have influenced and contributed to the development of this fantastic project — "The Best Jokes on Earth" — is too long to mention everyone; however, I wish to express my sincere thanks and appreciation to each of you for your help.

There are a few individuals who deserve special recognitions for their labor of love, terrific sense of humor, and special contributions.

To my lovely and multitalented wife, Grace; her dad, Robert Lupfer; my good friend Larry Hoover; and Deb Dahrling – thank you for all your support, motivation and love. This book would not have been possible without you.

And to the readers, I wish to thank you and encourage each of you to share the love, joy and laughter here with all whom you encounter along the road of life.

May God bless you.

Mel Foster

CHAPTER 1: ADULT HUMOR

SPORTS FAN

While the football fan was thrilled to be at the Super Bowl, he was disappointed with the location of his seat. Peering across the stadium through his binoculars, he spied an empty seat on the 50-yard line and makes his way there.

He asked the man in the seat next to him, "May I sit there?"

"Sure," the man replied. "This was my wife's seat. She was a huge football fan, and we came to the games together all the time until she passes away." "I'm sorry for you loss," the man said, "But I'm curious. Why didn't you give the extra ticket to a friend or relative?"

The widower replied, "They're all at the funeral."

FRED'S FUNERAL

Last Wednesday evening, a stranger entered our church and asked to speak to the pastor. Ol' eagle-eyed Rev spotted him and replied, "I'm the Pastor, how may I help you?"

The stranger said, "My dog Fred died yesterday, and I'd like for you to have a funeral for him here."

"I'm sorry to hear about your dog Fred sir, but this is a Baptist church, we don't do funerals for dogs here," said the Pastor.

"Well Ol' Fred was just like a person, he'd been my best friend for over 20 years, come on reverend, could you say a few nice words at a eulogy for Fred?"

"I'm sorry sir, like I said, we Baptist's don't do funerals for dogs!"

"That's too bad Pastor, because I was going to donate $50,000 to your church."

As the stranger turned to leave, Ol' Rev touched him and said, "Hold on, why didn't you tell me Ol' Fred was a Baptist? I believe we can work something out!"

THE PRESCRIPTION

A woman goes to the drugstore and asks for arsenic.

"What do you want that for?" The Pharmacist asks.

"I want to kill my husband," she replied. "He's having an affair with another woman."

"I can't sell you arsenic to kill your husband," says the Pharmacist, "even if he is cheating."

The woman pulls out a picture of her husband with the Pharmacist's wife.

The druggist turns pale and replies, "Oh I didn't realize you had a prescription."

LADY AND THE LEXUS

A lady walked into a Lexus dealership to browse, and spotted the most beautiful, perfectly loaded Lexus and walked over to inspect it closer. As she bent forward to feel the fine leather upholstery, an unexpected little burst of flatulence escaped her. Very embarrassed, she anxiously looked around to see if anyone had noticed.

Sure enough, there standing behind her was a salesman. With a pleasant smile he greeted her. "Good day, madam. How may we help you today?"

Trying to maintain an air of sophistication and acting as though nothing had happened, she smiled back and asked, "Sir what is the price of this lovely vehicle?"

Still smiling pleasantly, he replied, "Madam I'm very sorry to say! If you farted just touching it, you're going to shit when you hear the price."

MR. SCHWARTZ

A mortician was working late one night. It was his job to examine the dead bodies before they were sent off to be buried or cremated. As he examined the body of Mr. Schwartz, who was about to be cremated, he made an amazing discovery. Schwartz had the longest private part he had ever seen!

"I'm sorry Mr. Schwartz," said the mortician, "but I can't send you off to be cremated with a tremendously huge private part like this. It has to be saved

4

for posterity." With that, the coroner used his tools to remove the dead man's scaling. He stuffed his prize into a briefcase and took it home.

The first person he showed it to was his wife.

"I have something to show you that you won't believe," he said and opened up his briefcase.

"Oh my God!" the wife screamed. "Schwartz is dead!"

THE LOVE DRESS

A woman stopped by at her recently married son's house. She rang the doorbell and walked in. She was shocked to see her daughter-in-law lying on the couch, totally naked. Soft music was playing, and the aroma of perfume filled the room.

"What are you doing?" She asked.

"I'm waiting for my husband to come home from work," the daughter-in-law answered.

"But you're naked!" The mother-in-law exclaimed.

"This is my love dress," The daughter-in-law said.

"Love dress? But you're naked!"

"My husband loves me to wear this dress," she explained. "It excites him to no end. Every time he sees me in this dress, he instantly becomes romantic and ravages me for hours on end. He can't get enough of me."

The mother-in-law left. When she got home, she undressed, showered, put on her best perfume, dimmed the lights, put on a romantic CD, and lay on the couch waiting for her husband to arrive.

Finally, her husband came home. He walked in and saw her lying there so provocatively.

"What are you doing?" He asked.

"This is my love dress," she whispered, sensually.

"Needs ironing, he said. "What's for dinner?"

LOYALTY IN MARRIAGE

A woman's husband had been slipping in and out of a coma for several months, yet she had stayed by his bedside every single day.

One day he motioned for her to come nearer. As she sat by him, he whispered, his eyes full of tears, "You have been with me all through the bad times. When I got fired, you were there to support me. When my business failed, you were there. When we lost the house, you stayed right there. When my health started failing, you were still by my side…. You know what?"

"What dear?" She gently asked, smiling as her heart began to fill with warmth,

"I think you're bad luck. Get the fuck away from me!"

VERY SICK HUSBAND

A woman accompanied her husband to the doctor's office. After his checkup, the doctor called the wife into his office alone.

He said, "Your husband is suffering from a very severe disease, combined with horrible stress. If you don't do the following, your husband will surely die."

"Each morning, fix him a healthy breakfast. Be pleasant, and make sure he is in a good mood. For lunch make him a nutritious meal. For dinner, prepare an especially nice meal for him. Don't burden him with chores, as he probably had a hard day. Don't discuss your problems with him, it will only make his stress worse. And most importantly, make love with your husband several times a week and satisfy his every whim. If you can do this for the next 10 months to a year, I think your husband will regain his health completely."

On the way home the husband asked the wife, "What did the doctor say?"

"You're going to die," she replied.

WEDDING NIGHT

A young man married a beautiful woman who had previously divorced ten husbands. On their wedding night she told her new husband, "Please be gentle; I'm still a virgin."

"What?" Said the puzzled groom. "How can that be if you've been married ten times?"

"Well, husband #1 was a Sales Representative; he kept telling me how great it was going to be.

Husband #2 was in Software Services; he was never really sure how it was supposed to function, but he said he'd look into it and get back to me.

Husband #3 was from Field Services; he said everything checked out diagnostically, but he just couldn't get the system up.

Husband #4 was in Telemarketing; even though he had the order he didn't know when he would be able to deliver.

Husband #5 was an Engineer; he understood the basic process, but wanted three years to research, implement and design a new state-of-the-art method.

Husband #6 was from Administration; he thought he knew how, but he wasn't sure whether it was his job or not.

Husband #7 was in Marketing; although he had a product, he was never sure how to position it.

Husband #8 was a Psychiatrist; all he ever did was talk about it.

Husband #9 was a Gynecologist all he ever did was look.

Husband #10 was a Stamp Collector; all he did was......................... God I miss him!

But now that I've married you, I'm so excited!"

"Good," said the husband, "But why?"

"You're with the Government. This time I know I'm gonna get SCREWED!"

SHORT AND PRETTY

Sam was fixing a door and he found that he needed a new hinge, so he sent his wife, Mary to the hardware store. At the hardware store, Mary saw a beautiful teapot on a top shelf while she was waiting for Ted, the manager to finish waiting on a customer.

When Ted was finished, Mary asked, "How much for the teapot?"

Ted replied, "That's silver and it costs $100!"

"My goodness, that sure is a lotta money!" Mary exclaimed. Then she proceeded to describe the hinge that Sam had sent her to buy, and Ted went to the back room to find it.

From the back room Ted yelled, "Mary you wanna screw for that hinge?"

Mary replied, "No but I will for the teapot."

IRISH COFFEE

An Irish woman "of a certain age" visited her doctor to ask his help in reviving her husband's sex drive.

"What about trying Viagra?" asks the doctor.

"Not a chance," she said. "He won't even take an aspirin."

"Not a problem," replied the doctor. "Drop it into his coffee. He won't even taste it. Give it a try and call me in a week to let me know how things went."

A week later she rang up the doctor, who directly inquired as to progress.

The poor dear exclaimed, "Oh faith, bejaysus and begorrah! 'Twas horrid! Just terrible, doctor!"

"Really? What happened?" asked the doctor.

"Well I did as you advised and slipped it in his coffee, didn't I? The effect was almost immediate. He jumped himself straight up, with a twinkle in his eye and with his pants a-bulging fiercely! With one swoop of his arm, he sent the cups and tablecloth flying, ripped me clothes to tatters and took me then and there, making wild, mad passionate love to me on the tabletop! It was a nightmare, I tell you!"

"Why so terrible?" asked the doctor. "Do you mean you didn't enjoy it?"

"Of course I did doctor! Indeed 'twas the best sex I've had in 25 years. But I'll never be able to show me face in Starbucks again!"

THE MIND OF A MARRIED WOMAN

A guy asks his wife, "Honey, how come you never tell me when the sex is great?"

She replies, "Because you're never here at the time."

A CROSS-COUNTRY DRIVE

A husband and his wife driving cross-country pull into a motel for the night. The next morning the clerk hands him a bill for $350.

"How is it $350?" The man asks.

"Sir we have the finest motel in all of Kansas," the clerk replied. "We have an Olympic-sized heated pool, a private gym, a state-of-the-start conference room, a nine-hole golf course, an award winning restaurant and nightly entertainment by the top entertainers in the world."

"That's great but we didn't any of those facilities," the man says.

"But, sir they were all made available to you during your stay."

Frustrated, the man writes a check.

"Sir, I'm afraid this check is only for $100," the clerk notes.

"Correct," the man says. "I charged you $250 for sleeping with my wife."

"But I didn't!" the clerk screams.

"Well," the man replies, "she was here all night and I would have let you, so goodbye."

WORKING GIRL

A man was sitting in a bar drooling over a hot woman in a mini skirt. He decides to get up to send her a drink, and not only does she get up and sit next to him, but they also have an amazing conversation.

Finally the woman says, "Look you seem like a really nice guy, so I have to tell you that I'm a working girl. I get $200 for what you think you're about to get for free."

"I have no problem with the money," the man replies, "but since you were so straightforward, I must tell you that when I come I go nuts; I bite, scratch, kick punch and plain ol' destroy the place."

"Oh my goodness!" the woman says. "How long does that last?"

"Until I get my $200 back," he replies.

BLUE PAJAMAS

A man calls home to his wife and says, "Honey, I have been asked to go fishing up in Canada with my boss and several of his friends. We'll be gone for a week. This is a good opportunity for me to get that promotion I've been wanting, so could you please pack enough clothes for a week and set out my rod and tackle box? We're leaving from the office and I will swing by the house and pick up my things.

"Oh! And please pack my new blue silk pajamas."

The wife thinks this sounds a bit fishy, but being the good wife she is, she does exactly what her husband asked.

The following weekend he came home a little tired, but otherwise looking good. The wife welcomes him home and asks if he caught many fish.

He says, "Yes! Lots of walleyes, some blue gill, and even a few pike. But why didn't you pack my new blue silk pajamas like I asked you to?"

The wife replies, "I did, they're in your tackle box."

KNOW YOUR NEIGHBOR

A married couple is walking past their neighbor's house. "John and Sarah are so loving towards each other," says the wife. "Every time he sees her he gives her a big kiss, unlike someone I know."

"Hey, I'd love to," says the husband, "but I don't know her that well."

GO FLY A KITE

A husband in his back yard is trying to fly a kite. He throws the kite up in the air, the wind catches it for a few seconds, and then it comes crashing back down to earth. He tries this a few times with no success.

All the while, his wife is watching from the kitchen window, muttering to herself how men need to be told how to do everything. She opens the window and yells to her husband, "You need a piece of tail!"

The man turns with a confused look on his face and says, "Make up your mind. Last night you told me to go fly a kite!"

THE WEDDING TEST

My girlfriend and I had been dating for over a year when we decided to get married. My parents helped us in every way, and my friends encouraged me.

My girlfriend? She was a dream! There was one thing bothering me. That one thing was her younger sister.

My prospective sister-in-law was 20 years of age, and wore tight miniskirts and low-cut blouses. She would regularly bend down when near me, and I got many pleasant views of her underwear. It had to be deliberate. She never did it when she was near anyone else.

One day, little sister calls and asked me to come over to check the wedding invitations. She was alone when I arrived. She whispered to me that soon I was to be married, and she had feelings and desires for me that she could not overcome, and did not really want to overcome. She told me that she wanted to make love to me just once before I got married and committed my life to her sister.

I was in total shock and could not say a word. She said, "I'm going upstairs to my bedroom and if you want to go ahead with it just come up and get me."

I was stunned. I was frozen in shock as I watch her go up the stairs. When she reached the top, she pulled down her panties and threw them down the stairs at me. I stood there for a moment, then turned and went straight for the front door. I opened the door and stepped out of the house and walked straight toward my car. My future father-in-law was standing outside. With tears in his eyes he hugged me and said, "We are very happy that you have passed our little test. We could not ask for a better man for our daughter. Welcome to the family!"

The moral of the story is … always keep your condoms in your car.

TIDE

A man with no arms or legs is sunbathing on the beach. He is approached by three beautiful young women who take pity on him.

The first woman says to him, "Have you ever been hugged?"

The man shakes his head, and she leans down and gives him a big hug.

The second woman says to him, "Have you ever been kissed?"

He shakes his head and she kisses him.

Rather abruptly, the third woman asks, "Have you ever been fucked?"

"No," says the man, his eyes lighting up.

"Well, you are now. The tide's coming in!"

GAY COWBOY

A successful rancher died and left everything to his devoted wife.

She was a very good-looking woman and determined to keep the ranch, but knew very little about ranching, so she decided to place an ad in the newspaper for a ranch hand.

Two cowboys applied for the job. One was gay and the other a drunk.

She thought long and hard about it, and when no one else applied she decided to hire the gay guy, figuring it would be safer to have him around the house than the drunk.

He proved to be a very hard worker who put in long hours every day and know a lot about ranching. For weeks the two of them worked, and the ranch was doing very well.

Then one day the rancher's widow said to the hired hand, "You have done a really good job, and the ranch looks great. You should go into town and kick up your heels."

The hired hand readily agreed and went into town one Saturday night.

One o'clock came, and he didn't return. Two o'clock and no hired hand. He returned around 2:30, and upon entering his room, he found the rancher's widow sitting by the fireplace with a glass of wine, waiting for him.

She quietly called him over to her, and said, "Unbutton my blouse and take it off."

Trembling, he did as she directed.

"Now take off my boots."

He did as she asked, ever so slowly.

"Now take off my socks."

He removed each gently and placed them neatly by her boots.

"Now take off my skirt."

He slowly unbuttoned it, constantly watching her eyes in the firelight.

"Now take off my bra."

Again, with trembling hands, he did as he was told and dropped it to the floor.

"Now," she said, "Take off my panties."

By the light of the fire, he slowly pulled them down and off.

Then she looked at him and said, "If you ever wear my clothes into town again, you're fired!"

THE PASTOR'S ASS

The pastor entered his donkey in a race and it won. The pastor was so pleased with the donkey that he entered it in the race again, and it won again. The local paper read: PASTOR'S ASS OUT FRONT.

The bishop was so upset with this kind of publicity that he ordered the pastor not to enter the donkey in another race. The next day, the local paper headline read: BISHOP SCRATCHES PASTOR'S ASS.

This was too much for the bishop, so he ordered the pastor to get rid of the donkey. The pastor decided to give it to a nun in a nearby convent.

The local paper, hearing of the news, posted the following headline the next day: NUN HAS BEST ASS IN TOWN.

The bishop fainted. He informed the nun that she would have to get rid of the donkey, so she sold it to a farmer for $10.

The next day the paper read: NUN SELLS ASS FOR $10.

This was too much for the bishop, so he ordered the nun to buy back the donkey and lead it to the plains where it could run wild.

The next day the headlines read: NUN ANNOUNCES HER ASS IS WILD AND FREE.

The bishop was buried the next day.

The moral of the story is … being concerned about public opinion can bring you much grief and misery … and even shorten your life. So be yourself and enjoy life … stop worrying about everyone else's ass and you'll be a lot happier and live longer!

CLOSE SHAVE

A cowboy walked into a barbershop, sat in the barber's chair and said, "I'll have a shave and a shoe shine." The barber began to lather his face while a woman with the biggest, firmest, most beautiful breasts that he had ever seen knelt down and began to shine his shoes.

The cowboy said, "Young lady, you and I should go and spend some time in a hotel room."

She replied, "I'm married and my husband wouldn't like that."

The cowboy said, "Tell him you're working overtime and I'll pay you the difference."

She said, "You tell him. He is the one shaving you."

A PIOUS MAN

A pious man who had reached the age of 105 suddenly stopped going to synagogue. Alarmed by the old fellow's absence after so many years of faithful attendance the Rabbi went to see him.

He found him in excellent health, so the Rabbi asked, "How come after all these years we don't see you at services anymore?"

The old man looked around and lowered his voice. "I'll tell you Rabbi," he whispered. "When I got to be 90, I expected God to take me any day. But then I got to be 95, then 100, then 105. So I figured that God is very busy and must've forgotten about me, and I don't want to remind Him!"

OL' FRED

Ol' Fred had been a faithful Christian and was in the hospital, near death. The family called their preacher to stand with them. As the preacher stood next to the bed, ol' Fred's condition appeared to deteriorate and he motioned frantically for something to write on. The pastor lovingly handed him a pen and a piece of paper, and ol' Fred used his last bit of energy to scribble a note, then suddenly died.

The preacher thought it was best not to look at the note at the time, so he placed it in his jacket pocket. At the funeral, as he was finishing the message, he realized that he was wearing the same jacket that he was wearing when ol' Fred died. He said, "You know, ol' Fred handed me a note just before he died. I haven't looked at it, but knowing Fred, I'm sure there's a word of inspiration there for us all."

He opened the note, and read, "Please step to the left — you're standing on my oxygen tube!"

CHAPTER 2: ANIMAL HUMOR

MONKEY BUSINESS

A couple is on a safari in Africa when the woman is abducted by a gorilla. Two weeks later she's found naked and alone, crying hysterically.

Her husband asks, "Did that mean ape hurt you?"

"He sure did!" the wife sobs. "Four days ago he fled to the hills, he hasn't called me, hasn't written."

SMART DOG

A man visits his local theatre. During the film he notices that a man has brought his dog along to watch — and what's more, the hound is laughing and crying in all the right places. The film finishes and the man wanders over to the pair.

"I couldn't help but notice your dog laughed at the funny lines and cried at the sad parts in the movie," the man says. "It's incredible."

"I can't believe it either," the dog owner replies. "He hated the book."

THE HORSE

A man was driving though west Texas one spring evening. The road was deserted and he had not seen a soul for what seemed like hours.

Suddenly his car started to cough and sputter and the engine slowly died away, leaving him sitting on the side of the road in total silence. He popped the hood and looked to see if there was anything that he could do to get it going again. Unfortunately, he had a limited knowledge of cars, so all he could do was look at the engine, feeling despondent.

As he stood looking at the gradually fading light of his flashlight, he cursed that he had not put in new batteries, like he had promised himself. Suddenly, through the inky shadows, came a deep voice. "It's your fuel pump."

The man raised up quickly, striking his head on the underside of the hood. "Who said that?" he demanded.

There were two horses standing in the fenced field alongside the road and the man was amazed when the nearest of the two horses repeated, "It's your fuel pump. Tap it with your flashlight, and try it again."

Confused, the man tapped the fuel pump with his key and sure enough the engine roared to life. He muttered a short thanks to the horse and screeched away. When he reached the next town, he ran into the local bar. "Gimme a large whiskey, please!" he said.

A rancher sitting at the bar looked at the man's ashen face and asked, "What's wrong man? You look like you've seen a ghost!"

"It's unbelievable," the man said, and recalled the whole tale to the rancher.

The rancher took a sip of his beer and look thoughtful. "A horse, you say? Was it by any chance a white horse?"

The man replied to the affirmative. "Yes, it was! Am I crazy?"

"No you ain't crazy! In fact, you're lucky," said the rancher, "because that black horse don't know shit about cars!"

CUTS LIKE A KNIFE

A frog telephones a psychic hot line and asks about his love life.

"You are going to meet a beautiful young woman who will want to get to know the inner you," the psychic predicts.

"That's great," says the frog. "When will I meet her?"

"Next year in Biology class."

HAPPY COMPANIONS

A man is walking down the street and sees a penguin. He wants to do the right thing so he takes the penguin to the police station and says to the desk sergeant, "I found this penguin at the bus stop. What should I do with it?"

The desk sergeant says, "Take it to the zoo."

The guy does.

Two weeks later the desk sergeant spots the same guy and the penguin at the bus stop, and says, "I thought I told you to take that penguin to the zoo?"

"I did," says the man, "And we had so much fun we're going again this afternoon."

QUICK RABBITS

Four jackrabbits are strolling in the prairie. Out of nowhere, a gang of coyotes began to chase them, so the rabbits ran under a huge cactus for refuge.

Then the hungry coyotes surrounded the cactus.

One jackrabbit says to the others, "Okay, should we run for it or wait until we outnumber them?"

SHARP VETERINARIAN

Dr. Lupfer is the local veterinarian, known for his wry humor. He surpassed himself one summer day when a city dog was brought to him after an encounter with a porcupine.

After almost an hour of prying, pulling, cutting and stitching, he returned the dog to its owner, who asked what she owed.

"Fifteen dollars, ma'am," he answered.

"Why that's simply outrageous!" she stormed. "That's what's wrong with you Maine people, you are always trying to overcharge summer visitors. Whatever do you do in the winter when we're not being gypped here?"

"Raise porcupines, ma'am."

RELIGIOUS SQUIRRELS

Squirrels had overrun three churches in town. After much prayer, the elders of the first church determined that the animals were pre-destined to be there. Who were they to interfere with God's will, they reasoned. Soon, the squirrels multiplied.

The elders of the second church decided they couldn't harm any of God's creatures, so they humanely trapped the squirrels and set them free outside of town. Three days later the squirrels were back.

It was only the third church that succeeded in keeping the pests away. The elders baptized the squirrels and registered them as members of the Church. Now they only see them on Christmas and Easter.

DIRTY BIRD

Dave gets a parrot for his birthday. It has a bad attitude, and a worse vocabulary. Every other word is a swear word. Dave tries to change the bird's behavior with polite words, soft music, but nothing works.

Out of desperation, he throws the bird in the freezer. It squawks, kicks, screams, then falls silent. Worried, Dave swings the freezer door open.

The parrot calmly steps out and says, "I believe I may have offended you with my rude language and actions. I will endeavor at once to correct my behavior."

Dave is astonished at the change in the bird's attitude and is about to ask what caused it, when the parrot continues.

"May I ask what the chicken did?"

MAN'S BEST FRIEND

A couple of dog owners are arguing about whose dog is smarter.

"My dog is so smart," says the first owner, "that every morning he waits for the paperboy to come around. He tips the kid, then brings the paper to me, along with my morning coffee."

"I know," said the second owner.

"How do you know?"

"My dog told me."

DUCKS

Three women die together in an accident and go to Heaven.

When they get there, St. Peter says, "We only have one rule here in Heaven: Don't step on the ducks!"

So they enter Heaven, and sure enough there are ducks all over the place. It is almost impossible not to step on a duck, and although they try their best to avoid them, the first woman accidentally steps on one.

Along comes St. Peter with the ugliest man she ever saw. St. Peter chains them together and says, "Your punishment for stepping on a duck is to spend eternity chained to this ugly man!"

The next day, the second woman accidentally steps on a duck and along comes St. Peter, who doesn't miss a thing. With him is another extremely ugly man. He chains them together with the same admonishment as for the first woman.

The third woman has observed all this, and not wanting to be chained for all eternity to an ugly man, is very, VERY careful where she steps.

She manages to go months without stepping on any ducks, but one day St. Peter comes up to her with the most handsome man she has ever laid eyes on.... Very tall, long eyelashes, muscular and thin.

St. Peter chains them together without saying a word.

The happy woman says, "I wonder what I did to deserve being changed to you for all of eternity?"

The guy says, "I don't know about you, but I stepped on a duck!"

THERE'S NO PLACE LIKE HOME

Bookie disliked the family cat and decided to get rid of it. He drove the feline 20 blocks from home and left it, but when he pulled into his driveway, there was the cat.

The next day he left the kitty 40 blocks away, but again, the cat beats him home. So he took the cat on a long drive, arbitrarily turning left, then right and making U-turns, anything to throw off the cat's keen sense of direction before abandoning him in a park across town.

Hours later, he called his wife. "Martha, is the cat there?"

"Yes," she replied, "Why?"

"Put him on the phone. I'm lost and I need directions home."

CAGED HEAT

A small zoo in Alabama acquires a rare gorilla who quickly becomes agitated. The zookeeper determines that the female ape is in heat, but there are no male apes available for mating.

The zookeeper approaches a redneck janitor with a proposition. "Would you be willing to have sex with this gorilla for $500?" he asks.

The janitor accepts the offer, but only on three conditions. "First, I don't want to have to kiss her. And second, you can never tell anyone about this."

The zookeeper agrees to the conditions and asks about the third condition.

"Well," says the janitor, "I'm gonna need another week to come up with the $500."

THE DRUNK AND THE SQUIRREL

A man is sitting at the bar drinking away his sorrows. Suddenly, he sees two squirrels burst through the front door and sit down next to him.

Amazed, the man watches as they order drinks, and eat from a bowl of nuts. Finally the man gives up on trying to contain his curiosity.

"Where did you two learn to talk?" he asks.

"Wow, you're drunk," the squirrel closest to him replies. "There's only one of me."

DEAD MULE IN THE CHURCHYARD

A pastor went to his church office on Monday morning and discovered a dead mule in the churchyard. He telephoned the police. Since there did not appear to be any foul play, the police referred the pastor to the Health Department. They explained, "Since there is no health threat, you need to call the Sanitation Department."

When the pastor called the Sanitation Department, the manager said, "I can't pick up the dead mule without authorization from the mayor."

The pastor was not at all too eager to call the mayor, who possessed a very bad temper and was always extremely unpleasant and hard to deal with, but eventually the pastor called the mayor anyway.

The mayor did not disappoint the pastor.

The mayor immediately began to rant.

After his continued rant at the pastor, the mayor finally asked, "Why did you call me anyway? Isn't it your job to bury the dead?"

The pastor paused for a brief prayer, and asked the Lord to direct his response.

The Lord led the pastor to the words he was seeking.

"Well, yes, mayor, it IS my job to bury the dead, BUT I always like to notify the next of kin first!"

THE BEAR AND THE GRASSHOPPER

A bear walks into a bar and says, "I'd like a beer … … … and some of those peanuts."

The bartender asks, "Sure, but why the big paws?"

>>

A grasshopper hops into a bar. The bartender says, "You're quite a celebrity around here. We've even got a drink named after you."

The grasshopper asks, "You've got a drink named Steve?"

HORSE BAR

A guy walks into a bar and there's a horse serving drinks. The horse asks, "What are you staring at? Haven't you ever seen a horse tending bar?"

The guy says, "It's not that. I just never thought the parrot would sell the place."

THE PANDA

A panda walks into a bar, sits down, and orders a sandwich. He eats, pulls out a gun and shoots the waiter dead. As the panda stands up to go, the bartender shouts, "Hey! Where are you going? You just shot my waiter and you didn't pay for the food."

The panda yells back, "Hey man, I'm a panda. Look it up!"

The bartender opens his dictionary to **PANDA:** "A tree-climbing mammal of Asian origin, characterized by distinct black-and-white coloring. Eats shoots and leaves."

COMICAL CANINE

A poodle and a collie were walking down the street. The poodle turned to the collie and complained, "My life is a mess. My owner is mean, my girlfriend is having an affair with a German shepherd, and I'm nervous as a cat."

"Why don't you go see a psychiatrist?" asked the collie.

"I can't," replied the poodle, "I'm not allowed on the couch."

>>

Q: Why are dogs such bad dancers?

A: They have two left feet.

NEXT TIME, STAY IN A HOTEL

Two campers are hiking in the woods when one of them is bitten on the rear end by a rattlesnake.

"I'll go into town for a doctor," the other says. He runs 10 miles to a small town and finds the only doctor delivering a baby.

"I can't leave," the doctor says. "But here's what to do. Take a knife, cut a little X where the bite is, suck out the poison and spit it to the ground."

The guy runs back to his friend, who is in agony.

"What did the doctor say?" the victim cries.

"He says you're gonna die."

CHAPTER 3: ATTORNEY HUMOR

AN HONEST LAWYER

An independent woman started her own business. She was shrewd and diligent, so business kept coming in. Pretty soon she realized she needed in-house counsel, and so she began interviewing young lawyers.

"As I'm sure you can understand," she stated to one of the first applicants, "in a business like this, our personal integrity must be beyond question." She leaned forward. "Mr. Robinson, are you an 'honest' lawyer?"

"Honest?" replied the job prospect. "Let me tell you something about honest. Why I'm so honest that my dad lent me $15,000 for my education and I paid back every penny the minute I tried my very first case."

"Impressive. And what sort of case was that?"

He squirmed in his seat and admitted, "My dad sued me for the money."

HAPPY DAYS

A guy calls a law office and says, "I want to talk to my lawyer."

The receptionist replies, "I'm sorry, but he died last week."

The next day he phones again and asks the same question. The receptionist replies, "I told you yesterday that he died last week."

The next day the guy calls again and asks to speak to his lawyer. By this time the receptionist is getting angry and says, "I keep telling you, your lawyer died last week. Why do you keep calling?"

The guy says, "Because I just love hearing it."

LAWYER IN HEAVEN

A lawyer died. At the same moment, the pope also died. They arrived at the same moment. They spend the day in orientation, and as they're getting in their heavenly vestments, the pope gets a plain white toga and wings, like everyone else, and the lawyer gets much finer apparel, made of gold thread, and Gucci shoes.

Then they get to where they're going to live. The pope gets what everyone else gets, a replica of a Holiday Inn room, and the lawyer gets an 18-room mansion with servants and a swimming pool.

At dinnertime, the pope receives the standard meal, a Manischewitz kosher TV dinner, and the lawyer receives a fine and tasty meal, served on silver platters.

By this time, the lawyer is beginning to suspect that an error has been made, so he asks one of the angels in charge. "Has there been some kind of mistake? This guy was the pope, and he gets what everyone else gets, and I'm just a lawyer and I'm getting the finest of everything!"

The angel replied, "No mistake, sir. We've had lots of popes here, but you're the first lawyer we've ever had."

THREE QUESTIONS

A new client had just come in to see a famous lawyer. "Can you tell me how much you charge?"

"Of course," the lawyer replied. "I charge $300 to answer three questions."

"Well that's a bit steep isn't it?"

"Yes, it is," said the lawyer. "And what's your third question?"

FAMILY HEIRS

A lawyer meets with the family of a recently deceased millionaire for the reading of the will.

"To my loving wife, Louise, who always stood by me, I leave the house and two million dollars," the attorney reads. "To my darling daughter, Katherine, who looked after me in sickness and kept the business going, I leave the yacht, the business, and one million dollars."

"And finally," the lawyer concludes, "to my cousin, Ron, who hated me, argued with me, and thought I would never mention him in my will, well, you were wrong. HI RON!"

THE FISHING TRIP

One Saturday morning an old attorney gets up early, dresses quietly, gets his lunch made, puts on his long johns, grabs the dog and goes to the garage to hook up his boat to the truck, and down the driveway he goes.

As he gets to the street he realizes it's worse than he thought: there is snow mixed in with the rain, and the wind is blowing 50 mph.

Minutes later, he returns to the garage. He comes back into the house and turns on the TV to the weather channel. He finds it's going to be bad weather all day long, so he puts his boat back in the garage, quietly undresses and slips back into bed.

There he cuddles up to his wife's back, now with a different anticipation and whispers, "The weather out there is terrible."

To which she sleepily replies, "And can you believe my stupid husband is out there fishing in that crap?"

AT FIRST GLANCE

A man walks into a bar. He sees a beautiful, well-dressed woman sitting on a bar stool alone. He walks up to her and says, "Hi there, how's it going tonight?"

She turns to him, looks him straight in the eye and says, "I'll screw anybody, anytime, anywhere, any place. It doesn't matter to me."

The guy raises his eyebrows and asks, "No kidding? What law firm do you work for?"

SELF-EMPLOYED LIAR

I love working for myself; it's so empowering, except when I call in sick. I always know I'm lying!

SWIMMING WITH SHARKS

Q: What do you get when you cross a librarian and a lawyer?

A: All the information you want, except you can't understand it.

WHAT'S WRONG WITH LAWYER JOKES

Q: What's wrong with lawyer jokes?

A: Lawyers don't think they're funny, and nobody else seems to think that they're jokes.

PSYCHIATRY AT ITS BEST

Visiting the psychiatry ward, an attorney asked how doctors decide to institutionalize a patient.

"Well," the director said, "we fill a bathtub, then offer a teaspoon, a teacup and a bucket to the patient, and ask him to empty the tub."

"I get it," the attorney said. "A normal person would use the bucket because it's the biggest."

"No," the director said. "A normal person would pull the plug."

EDITOR-IN-CHIEF

An attorney, doctor, and newspaperman were deep in the jungle on a safari when they were captured by cannibals.

"Oh yes," the chief of the tribe exclaimed.

"We're going to put you all into a big pot of water, cook you and eat you."

"You can't do that," the tour leader said. "I'm the editor of the New York Times."

"Well," the chief responded. "Tonight you'll be 'EDITOR-IN-CHIEF!' "

THE GENEROUS FAMILY LAW JUDGE

"Mr. Hardaway, I have reviewed this case very carefully," the divorce court judge said, "and I've decided to give your wife $775 a week."

"That's very generous and fair of you, Your Honor," the husband said. "And every now and then I'll try to send her a few bucks myself."

DEAD JUDGE

A family law attorney telephoned the governor just after midnight, insisting that he talk to him regarding a matter of utmost urgency. An aide eventually agreed to wake up the governor.

"So what is it?" grumbled the governor.

"Judge Graber has just died," said the attorney, "and I want to take his place."

The governor replied, "Well, it's okay with me if it's okay with the undertaker."

A CHANGE OF VENUE

An attorney passed on and found himself in Heaven, but was not at all happy with his accommodations. He complained to St. Peter, who told him his only course of action was to appeal. The lawyer immediately appealed and was told it would take three years to hear his appeal. The attorney protested that this was unconscionable, but to no avail.

The lawyer was then approached by the devil who told him that he could have the appeal heard within a few days if the lawyer would change the venue to Hell. When the lawyer asked why appeals were heard so much sooner in Hell, he was told, "We have all the judges."

BEASTS VS. ATTORNEY

On a trip together, a Hindu, a rabbi and a lawyer stop at a farmhouse and ask to stay the night.

"There's space for two, but one will have to sleep in the barn," said the farmer.

"I'll go," the Hindu volunteers. A few minutes later, the lawyer and the rabbi hear a knock.

"There's a cow in the barn," the Hindu says. "A cow is sacred, and I cannot sleep with a sacred beast."

"No problem, I can do it," the rabbi says, grabbing his pillow. But minutes later the rabbi knocks.

"There's a pig in the barn. It's an unclean animal and my belief forbids me to be near such a creature."

With a tired sigh, the lawyer heads out. Almost immediately there's a third knock at the door.

It's the cow and pig.

ALWAYS TELL THE TRUTH

Family law judge to mother: Do you understand that you have sworn to tell the truth?

Mother: I do.

Judge: Do you understand what will happen if you are not truthful?

Mother: Sure. I get everything I want.

ASSHOLES AREN'T ALWAYS JUDGES

A father fresh from another irrational court ruling comes into a bar. Angrily he shouts, "I think all family court judges are assholes!"

A slurred response from the back of the bar is heard.

"I resent that!"

The father peers into the back and asks, "Why, are you a family court judge?"

"No," the voice slurs, "I'm an asshole."

CONTEMPT OF COURT

Father (after being denied access to his children and having all his asses seized): "Can I address the court?"

Judge: "Of course."

Father: "If I call you a son of a bitch, what would you do?"

Judge: "I'll hold you in contempt and sentence you to five days in jail."

Father: "What if I thought you were a son of a bitch?"

Judge: I can't do anything about that. There's no law against thinking."

Father: "In that case, I think you're a son of a bitch."

QUICK COURT QUIPS

Q: What happens when you cross a pig with a family court judge?

A: Nothing. There are some things a pig just won't do!

>>

Q: What do you call a judge gone bad?

A: Senator.

>>

Q: What do you call a lawyer gone bad?

A: Your Honor.

>>

Q: What's the difference between a dead skunk and a dead family court judge in the road?

A: Vultures will eat the skunk.

>>

Q: You're trapped in a room with a tiger, a rattlesnake and a family law judge. Your gun only has two bullets. What should you do?

A: Shoot the judge. Twice.

>>

Q: Did you hear that the Post Office just recalled their latest stamps?

A: They had pictures of the Court of Appeal judges on them ... and people couldn't figure out which side to spit on.

>>

Q: Your family court judge and you ex-mother-in-law are trapped in a burning building. You have time to save only one of them. Do you have lunch or go to a movie?

CHAPTER 4: CHILD HUMOR

SIX FEET UNDER

Little Susie is in her back yard filling a big hole with dirt, occasionally smacking it with a shovel.

Her curious neighbor peers over the fence, and asks, "What are you doing, Susie?"

"I'm burying my goldfish," she replies tearfully.

"Oh, I'm sorry," he says, "but isn't that an awfully big hole for a goldfish?"

Susie pats the last heap of dirt, looks up and says, "That's because he's inside your damn cat!"

FIRST GRADE

A teacher asked her first-grade class to use the word "lovely" twice in a short story to demonstrate that they understand its meaning.

"Mary, let's hear from you first." the teacher says.

"On the weekend my mommy made some lovely cakes," Mary says. "My family and I ate them and they tasted lovely."

"Thank you, Mary, that was very good," the teacher says.

"And how about you, Sam? Can you use the word lovely two times in the same story?"

"I sure can, ma'am," Sam replies. "My big sister came home crying last night and told my daddy that she was going to marry the man with the motorcycle, and that she was pregnant with his baby."

After that my daddy said to her, "Well, that's lovely. That's just fucking lovely!"

POWER WATER

A little boy was sitting on the curb with a gallon of turpentine and shaking it up and watching all the bubbles.

A little while later, a priest came along and asked the little boy what he had.

The little boy replied, "This is the most powerful liquid in the world. It's called turpentine."

The priest said, "No, the most powerful liquid in the world is Holy Water. If you take some of this Holy Water and rub it on pregnant women's bellies, they'll pass healthy babies."

The little boy replied, "You take some of this here turpentine and rub it on a cat's ass and he'll pass a Harley-Davidson!"

EMERGENCY DELIVERY

Due to a power outage at the time, only one paramedic responded to the call. The house was very, very dark, so the paramedic asked Katelyn, a 3-year-old girl, to hold a flashlight high over her mommy so he could see while he helped deliver the baby. Very diligently, Katelyn did as she was asked. Heidi pushed and pushed, and after a little while, Connor was born. The paramedic lifted him by his little feet and spanked him on his bottom.

Connor began to cry.

The paramedic then thanked Katelyn for her help and asked the wide-eyed girl what she thought about what she had just witnessed.

Katelyn quickly responded, "He shouldn't have crawled in there in the first place! Spank him again!"

DESSERT

A woman comes home with two buckets of manure for the garden.

"What's that for?" asks her 5-year-old daughter.

"The strawberries," says her mom.

The girl stares at the buckets for a few moments, looks up and asks, "Can I just have mine with whipped cream?"

LEARNING CURVES

Two boys get their report card and notice that they both got F's from their sex-education teacher.

"I can't believe that we failed sex ed," says the first boy. "My dad's gonna kill me!"

"I know," says the other. "I'm so mad I could kick Mrs. Wilson in the nuts!"

CONNECTING ADULTS

Little Johnny and Susie are 10 years old, and in love. They want to get married, so Johnny asks his parents for their blessing. They think it's the most adorable thing.

"Where will the two of you live?" asks the father.

"In Susie's room." Johnny replies.

"Well, how are you planning to support her?" asks his mom.

"Her allowance plus mine makes $15 a week," says Johnny. "That's enough for two kids."

His mother smiles and says, "Sure, but what if you two have a baby?"

Johnny shrugs and says, "We've been lucky so far."

CHILD CURIOSITY

A mom is driving her little girl to a friend's house for a play date.

"Mommy," the little girl asks, "How old are you?"

"Honey, you are not supposed to ask a lady her age," the mother warns. "It is not polite."

"Okay," the little girl says. "How much do you weigh?"

"Now, really," the mother says. "These are very personal questions, and really none of your business."

Undaunted, the little girl asks, "Why did you and daddy get a divorce?"

"That is enough questions, honestly!" the exasperated mother walks away as the two friends begin to play.

"My mom won't tell me anything," the little girl says to her friend.

"Well," said the friend, "all you need to do is look at her driver's license. It is like a report card. It has everything on it."

Later that night, the little girl says to her mother, "I know how old you are. You are 32."

The mother is surprised and asks, "How did you find that out?"

"I also know that you weigh 140 pounds."

The mother is past surprise and shock now.

"How in Heaven's name did you find that out?"

"And," the little girl says triumphantly, "I know why you and daddy got a divorce."

"Oh really?" the mother asks. "And why's that?"

"Because you got an F in sex."

JOHNNY JOKES

A new teacher was trying to make use of her psychology courses. She started her class by saying, "Everyone who thinks they're stupid, stand up!"

After a few seconds, little Johnny stood up.

The teacher said, "Do you think you're stupid Johnny?"

"No ma'am, but I hate to see you standing there all by yourself!"

>>

Little Johnny watched, fascinated, as his mother smoothed cold cream on her face.

"Why do you do that mommy?" he asked.

"To make myself beautiful," said his mother, who then began removing the cream with a tissue.

"What's the matter?" Little Johnny asked. "Giving up?"

>>

The math teacher saw that Little Johnny wasn't paying attention in class. She called on him and said, "Johnny! What are 2 and 4 and 4 and 28 and 44?"

Little Johnny quickly replied, "NBC, CBS, HBO and the Cartoon Network!"

>>

At Sunday school, they were teaching how God created everything, including human beings.

Little Johnny, a child in the kindergarten class, seemed especially intent when they told him how Eve was created out of one of Adam's ribs.

Later in the week his mother noticed him lying down as though he were ill, and said, "Johnny, what is the matter?"

Little Johnny responded, "I have a pain in my side. I think I'm going to have a wife."

SURPRISE AT DINNER

One night, a wife cooks up some deer steaks and serves them to her husband and two children.

As they're enjoying the dinner, the husband thinks it'll be fun to have the children guess what type of meat they're eating.

"Is it beef?" Little Katie asks.

"Nope."

"Is it pork?" Little Willie asks.

"Nope."

"Heck, we don't know what it is, Dad," Willie exclaims.

"I'll give you a clue," the dad says as he smiles lovingly at his wife. "It's what mom sometimes calls me."

"Spit it out, Willie," Katie shouts, "We're eating asshole!"

KIDS ARE QUICK

Teacher: Maria, go to the map and find North America.

Maria: Here it is.

Teacher: Correct. Now class, who discovered America?

Class: Maria.

>>

Teacher: Why are you late, Frank?

Frank: Because of the sign.

Teacher: What sign?

Frank: The one that says, "School ahead, go slow."

>>

Teacher: John, why are you doing your math multiplication on the floor?

John: You told me to do it without using tables.

>>

Teacher: Glenn, how do you spell "crocodile?"

Glenn: K-R-O-K-O-D-I-A-L.

Teacher: No, that's wrong.

Glenn: Maybe it is wrong, but you asked me how I spell it.

>>

Teacher: Donald, what is the chemical formula for water?

Donald: HIJKLMNO

Teacher: What are you talking about?

Donald: Yesterday you said it's H to O.

>>

Teacher: Winnie, name one important thing we have today that we didn't have 10 years ago.

Winnie: Me!

>>

Teacher: Goss, why do you always get so dirty?

Goss: Well, I'm a lot closer to the ground than you are.

>>

Teacher: Millie, give me a sentence starting with "I".

Millie: I is....

Teacher: No Millie. Always say "I am."

Millie: Alright. "I am the ninth letter of the alphabet."

>>

Teacher: George Washington not only chopped down his father's cherry tree, but also admitted it. Now, Louie, do you know why his father didn't punish him?

Louie: Because he still had the axe in his hand.

>>

Teacher: Now, Simon, tell me frankly, do you say prayers before eating?

Simon: No, sir, I don't have to. My mom is a good cook.

>>

Teacher: Clyde, your composition on "My Dog" is exactly the same as your brother's. Did you copy him?

Clyde: No, teacher, it's the same dog.

>>

Teacher: Harold, what do you call a person who keeps on talking when people are no longer interested?

Harold: A teacher.

LADY AND THE BOY

A middle-aged woman sees a little boy standing on the corner, chain-smoking cigarettes and swigging freely from a bottle of beer.

Unable to bear it any longer, she walks up to him and asks, "Why aren't you in school today?"

"Damn, lady," the boy replies, "I'm only 4 years old!"

CONSTRUCTION KIDS

A young family moves next door to a construction site. The next morning a crew of builders arrive to work. Intrigued by the commotion, the family's 6-year-old daughter starts talking to the workers.

She hangs around every day and the builders take her under their wing, stopping to chat on their breaks and giving her small jobs to make her feel important.

At the end of the week the men are so charmed by their little friend that they chip in and give her $5.

The little girl's mom is impressed at her daughter's windfall and asks where she got the money.

"I've been working construction, mommy," the little girl says. "Building the house next door."

"How wonderful," the mother says. "And will you be working next week?"

"Mommy, I will," her daughter replies. "As long as those worthless cocksuckers at the lumber yard bring us the fucking timber we ordered!"

HILLBILLY KID

Three third-graders — an Irish kid, an Italian kid, and a hillbilly kid — are on the playground at recess. One of them suggests that they play a new game.

"Let's see who has the biggest weenie," the Italian kid says.

"Okay," they all agree.

The Italian kid pulls down his zipper and whips it out.

"That's nothing," says the Irish kid. He whips his out. It is a couple of inches longer.

Not to be outdone, the hillbilly kid whips his out. It is by far the biggest.

That night, as they were sitting down at the table and eating dinner, the hillbilly kid's mother asks, "What did you do at school today?"

"Oh, we worked on a science project, had a math test and read out loud from a new book, and during recess my friends and I played a new game. It's called, 'Let's see who has the biggest weenie.' "

"What kind of game is that, honey?" asks the mother.

"Well, me, Anthony and Patrick each pulled out our weenies and I had the biggest! The other kids said it's because I'm a hillbilly. Is that true, Mom?"

Mom replied, "No honey, it's because you're 23."

UGLY SON

There was a middle-aged couple that had two stunningly beautiful teenage daughters. The couple decided to try one last time for the son they always wanted. After months of trying, the wife finally got pregnant and delivered a healthy baby boy nine months later.

The joyful father rushed into the nursery to see his new son. He took one look and was horrified to see the ugliest child he had ever seen. He went to his wife and told her there was no way he could be the father of that child. "Look at the two beautiful daughters I fathered!" Then he gave her a stern look and asked, "Have you been fooling around on me?"

"Not this time," she replied.

GRANDMA EXPLAINS

He'd been playing outside with the other kids for awhile when he came into the other house and asked, "Grandma, what is it called when people are sleeping in the same room and one is on top of the other?"

She was a little taken aback, but decided to tell him the truth.

"It's called sexual intercourse, darling."

Little Tony just said, "Oh, okay." And went back outside to talk and play with the other kids.

A few minutes later he came back in and said angrily, "Grandma, it is not called sexual intercourse! It's called bunk beds! And Jimmy's mom wants to talk to you."

BOY AND THE BUCKET

A man is watching the parade in town and he's dying to take a leak. The line for the toilets is long, but the man notices a hole in the fence and decides to put it to use. Midstream, something grabs his weenie.

"Give me $5 or we'll chop off your weenie," he hears. Terrified, the man throws the money over the fence and is released.

Curious, he peeks over and sees a 12-year-old kid holding the money and younger kid holding a bucket and a knife.

"You little bastard, how much have you made today?" the man asks the older kid.

"About $200," he answers.

"And what about you, little kid?"

"I haven't made a cent, mister," says the younger child, "but I do have a bucket full of cocks."

HARD LABOR

Three boys in a schoolyard are bragging about their fathers.

Billy says, "My dad scribbles a few words on a piece of paper, calls it a poem, and they give him $50."

Bobby says, "Oh yeah? My dad scribbles a few words on a piece of paper, calls it a song, and they give him $100."

Ricky says, "I've got you both beat. My dad scribbles a few words on a piece of paper, calls it a sermon, and it takes eight people to collect all the money."

TEST FOR BECOMING A CIA AGENT

The CIA had an opening for an assassin. After all the background checks, interviews and testing were done, there were three finalists – two men and a woman.

For the final test, the CIA agents took one of the men to a large metal door and handed him a gun. "We must know that you will follow your instructions, no matter what the circumstances. Inside this room, you will find your wife sitting in a chair. Kill her." The man said, "You can't be serious. I could never shoot my wife."

The agent nodded and said, "Then you're not the right man for this job. Take your wife and go home."

The second man was given the same instructions. He took the gun and went into the room. All was quiet for about five minutes. Then the man came out with tears in his eyes. "I tried, but I can't kill my wife."

The agent nodded and said, "You don't have what it takes. Take your wife and go home."

Finally, it was the woman's turn. She was given similar instructions – to kill her husband. She took the gun and went into the room. Shots rang out, one after another.

Then they heard screaming, crashing, banging on the walls. The agent was just about to go in and see what was happening when the door opened and the woman stepped out, sweating profusely.

"This gun is loaded with blanks," she said. "I had to beat him to death with the chair."

LIVE AND LEARN

Psychiatry students were in their Emotional Extremes class. "Let's set some parameters," the professor said. "What's the opposite of joy?" he asked one student.

"Sadness," he replied.

"The opposite of depression," he asked another.

"Elation," came the reply.

"The opposite of woe?" he asked a girl from Texas.

She replied, "Sir, I believe that would be giddyup."

DIED IN SERVICE

One Sunday morning the pastor noticed little Alex standing in the foyer of the church staring up at a large plaque. It was covered with names with small American flags mounted on either side of it.

The 7-year-old had been staring at the plaque for some time, so the pastor walked up, stood behind the little boy, and said quietly, "Good morning, Alex."

"Good morning, Pastor," he replied, still focused on the plaque. "Pastor, what is this?" he asked.

The pastor said, "Well, son, it's a memorial to all the young men and women who died in the service."

Soberly, they just stood together, staring at the large plaque.

Finally, little Alex's voice, barely audible and trembling with fear, asked, "Which service, the 9:45 or 11:15?"

A TEACHABLE MOMENT

Teacher: Kids, what does the chicken give you?

Student: Meat!

Teacher: Very good! Now what does the pig give you?

Student: Bacon!

Teacher: Great! And what does the fat cow give you?

Student: Homework!

LITTLE LOGAN

Everyone was seated around the table as the food was being served. When little Logan received his plate, he started eating right away.

"Logan, wait until we say our prayer," his mother reminded him.

"I don't have to," the little boy replied.

"Of course you do," his mother insisted. "We say a prayer before eating at our house."

"That's at our house," Logan explained, "but this is Grandma's house and she knows how to cook."

CHAPTER 5: MORON

SIMPLE SIMON

Simple Simon applied for a deputy sheriff's job. In the interview, the sheriff asked him, "What's one and one?"

Simple Simon answered, "Eleven."

That's not what the sheriff meant, but he had to admit the boy was right.

Next question, "What two days of the week start with the letter 'T'?"

"Today and tomorrow."

The sheriff was impressed by the way Simon thought outside the box, so he challenged him. "Who killed Abraham Lincoln?"

Simon looked surprised and admitted, "I don't know."

"Well, go home and work on that for a while," replied the sheriff, satisfied that he had stumped him.

Simon went home and told his mother, "The interview went great! First day on the job and I'm already working on a murder case!"

NUNS AT A BASEBALL GAME

Sitting behind a couple of nuns at a baseball game (whose habits partially blocked the view), three men (Yankees fans) decided to badger the nuns in an effort to get them to move. In a very loud voice, the first guy said, "I think I'm going to Utah. There are only 100 nuns living there."

The second guy spoke up and said, "I want to go to Montana. There are only 50 nuns living there."

The third guy said, "I want to go to Idaho. There are only 25 nuns living there."

One of the nuns turned around, looked at the men, and in a very sweet, calm voice said, "Why don't you go to Hell... there aren't any nuns there."

BUSHWHACKED

Three Texas surgeons were playing golf together and discussing surgeries they had performed. One of them said, "I'm the best surgeon in Texas. A concert pianist lost seven fingers in an accident. I reattached them, and eight months later he performed a private concert for the Queen of England."

One of the others said, "That's nothing. A young man lost both arms and legs in an accident. I reattached them, and two years later he won a gold medal in the field events in the Olympics."

The third surgeon said, "You guys are amateurs. Several years ago a cowboy who was high on cocaine and alcohol rode a horse head-on into a trailer traveling 80 miles an hour. All I had left to work with was the horse's ass and a cowboy hat. Later he became the president of the United States."

STRANGERS ON THE PLANE

Two strangers are sitting in adjacent seats in an airplane. One guy says to the other, "Let's talk. I hear that the flight will go faster if you strike up a conversation with your fellow passenger."

The other guy, who had just opened a good book closes it slowly, takes off his glasses and asks, "What would you like to discuss?"

The first guy says, "Oh, I don't know. How about nuclear power?"

The other guy says, "OK, that could make for some pretty interesting conversation. But let me ask you a question first. A horse, a cow, and a deer all eat the same stuff, but the deer excretes pellets; the cow, big patties; and the horse, clumps of dried grass. Why is that?"

The first guy says, "I don't know."

The other guy says, "Oh? Well then, do you really feel qualified to discuss nuclear power when you don't know shit?"

BLONDE WITH A CELL PHONE

A young man wanted to get his beautiful blonde wife, Susie, something nice for their first wedding anniversary. So he decided to buy her a cell phone. He showed her the phone and explained to her all of its features. Susie was excited to receive the gift and simply adored her new phone.

The next day, Susie went shopping. Her phone rang, and to her astonishment, it was her husband on the other end.

"Hi Susie," he said. "How do you like your new phone?"

Susie replied, "I just love it! It's so small and your voice is clear as a bell, but there's one thing I don't understand …"

"What's that, Sweetie?" asked her husband.

"How did you know I was at Wal-Mart?"

BUBBA AND CLEM

One day, Clem was walking down Main Street when he saw his buddy Bubba driving a brand new pickup. Bubba pulled up to him with a wide grin.

"Bubba, where'd you get that truck?"

"Bobby Sue gave it to me," Bubba replied.

"She gave it to you? I knew she was kinda sweet on ya, but a new truck?"

"Well, Clem, let me tell you what happened. We were driving out on Count Road 6, in the middle of nowhere. Bobby Sue pulled off the road, put the truck in 4-wheel-drive, and headed into the woods. She parked the truck, got out, threw off all her clothes and said, 'Bubba take what you want!' So I took the truck!"

"Bubba, you're a smart man! Them clothes woulda never fit you!"

BUSTED

Two guys are busted for drugs. The judge declared, "I'd like to give you both a second chance. I want you to help others quit. Come back on Monday and I'll pass judgment then."

Next Monday, the judge asked the first guy, "How did you do?"

"Your Honor, I persuaded 17 people to give up drugs," he beamed.

"That's wonderful!" the judge said. "How did you do that?"

"I used a diagram to show two circles. One big one and one small one," the guy explained. "I said the big circle was your brain before drugs and the small one was your brain after."

"Very admirable! Not guilty!" said the judge, who then turned to the second man and asked, "How did you do?"

"Your Honor, I persuaded 156 people to give up drugs."

"Amazing! How?" the judge asked.

"Well, I used the same diagram. All I did was point to the smaller circle and said this is your asshole before you go to prison."

THE CHURCH

Finally! After 25 years on a deserted island, Joe was being rescued. As he climbed onto the boat, the curious crew noticed three small huts.

"What are those?" they asked.

"The first one is my home," Joe said, "and the second one is my church."

"What about the third hut?" the rescuers wanted to know.

"Oh," said Joe, "that's the church I used to belong to."

THE VOICE

A guy gets home from work one night and hears a voice in his head, which tells him, "Quit your job, sell your house, take your money, and go to Vegas."

The man is disturbed at what he hears and ignores the voice.

But the next day, the same thing happens. The voice tells him, "Quit your job, sell your house, take your money, go to Vegas."

Again the man ignores the voice, but he's becoming increasingly upset, and the third time he hears the voice, he succumbs to the pressure. He quits his job, sells his house, takes his money, and heads to Las Vegas.

The moment the man gets off the plane in Vegas, the voice tells him, "Go to Harrah's."

He hops in a cab and rushes over to the casino, where the voice tells him, "Go to the roulette table."

The man does as he is told.

When he gets to the roulette table, the voice tells him, "Put all your money on 17."

Nervously, the man cashes in all his money for chips and then puts them all on 17.

"Now watch," says the voice.

The dealer wishes the man good luck and spins the roulette wheel.

Around and around the ball caroms. The man anxiously watches the ball as it slowly loses speed, until it finally settles into number ... 21.

The voice says, "Fuck."

BUBBA'S TWO ASSHOLES

Bubba dies in a fire, and his body is brought to the morgue. The coroner calls in Bubba's two brothers to identify the charred body.

"Yep, he's burned pretty bad," says one of the brothers. "Roll him over."

"That ain't Bubba," says the other brother.

"Nope, it sure ain't," says the other brother.

"Bubba had two assholes!"

"What?" says the coroner, "I've never heard of such a thing."

"Yep," says the first brother, "Every time we'd go down to town, people'd say, 'Hey look, here comes Bubba with them two assholes.' "

HILLBILLY BIRTH

Deep in the back woods of Tennessee, a hillbilly's wife went into labor in the middle of the night, and the doctor was called out to assist in the delivery.

Since there was no electricity, the doctor handed the father-to-be a lantern and said, "Here, you hold this high so I can see what I'm doing!"

Soon a baby boy was brought into the world.

"Whoa there," said the doctor, "don't be in such a rush to put that lantern down. I think there's another one coming."

Sure enough, within minutes he had delivered a baby girl.

57

"Hold that lantern up, don't set it down, there's another one!" said the doctor.

Within a few minutes he had delivered a third baby.

"No, don't be in a hurry to put down that lantern, it seems there's yet another one coming!" cried the doctor.

The redneck scratched his head in bewilderment and asked the doctor, "You reckon it might be the light that's attractin' 'em?"

HILLBILLY HUNT

A hillbilly went hunting one day in Kentucky and bagged three ducks.

He put them in the bed of his pickup truck and was about to drive home when he was confronted by an ornery game warden who didn't like hillbillies.

The game warden ordered the hillbilly to show his hunting license, and the hillbilly pulled out a valid Kentucky hunting license.

The game warden looked at the license, then reached over and picked up one of the ducks, sniffed its butt, and said, "This duck ain't from Kentucky. This is a Tennessee duck. You got a Tennessee hunting license, boy?"

The hillbilly reached into his wallet and produced a Tennessee hunting license.

The game warden looked at it, then reached over and grabbed second duck, sniffed its butt, and said, "This ain't no Tennessee duck. This duck's from Mississippi. You got a Mississippi license?

The hillbilly reached into his wallet and produced a Mississippi hunting license.

The game warden then reached over and picked up the third duck, sniffed its butt, and said, "This ain't no Mississippi duck. This here duck's from South Carolina. You got a South Carolina hunting license?"

Again the hillbilly reached into his wallet and brought out a South Carolina hunting license.

"Boy, just where the hell is you from?"

The hillbilly turned around, dropped his pants, bent over, and said, "You tell me. You're the expert."

THAT'S MY BOY

A young Southern boy goes off to college, but about a third of the way through the semester he has foolishly squandered what money his parents had given him.

Then he gets an idea. He calls his daddy. "Dad," he says, "you won't believe the wonders that modern education are coming up with. Why, they actually have a program up here that will teach Ole Blue to talk!"

"That's absolutely amazing!" his father says. "How do I get him into that program?"

"Just send him down here with $1,000," the boy says. "I'll get him into the course."

So his father sends the dog and the $1,000. About two-thirds of the way through the semester the money runs out. The boy calls his father again.

"So how's Ole Blue doing, son?" his father asks.

"Awesome dad, he's talking up a storm," he says, "but you just won't believe this. They've had such good results with this program that they've implemented a new one to teach the animals how to read!"

"Read?" asks the father. "No kidding? What do I have to do to get him in that program?"

"Just send $2,500 and I'll get him in the class."

His father sends the money.

The boy has a problem. At the end of the year, his father will find out that the dog can neither talk nor read. So he shoots the dog.

When he gets home, his father is all excited.

"Where's Ole Blue? I just can't wait to see him talk and read something!"

"Dad," the boy says, "I have some grim news. This morning when I got out of the shower, Ole Blue was in the living room kicking back in the recliner, reading the morning paper, like he usually does. Then he turned to me and asked, "So is your daddy still messin' around with that little redhead who lives on Oak Street?"

The father says, "I hope you shot that son of a bitch before he told your mother!"

"I sure did, Dad!"

"That's my boy!"

KENTUCKY HANG GLIDER

Down in Kentucky you don't see too many people hang gliding. So, Bubba decided to save up and get a hang glider. He took it to the highest mountain, and after struggling to get to the top, he got ready to take flight. He took off running and when he got the edge – into the wind he went.

Meanwhile, Maw and Paw Hicks were sittin' on the porch talkin' 'bout the good ole days when Maw spotted the biggest bird she'd ever seen!

"Look at the size of that bird, Paw!" she exclaimed.

Paw raised up. "Get my gun, Maw!"

She ran into the house, brought out his pump shotgun. He took careful aim. BANG! … BANG! … BANG! … BANG! The monster-sized bird continued to sail silently over the treetops.

"I think ya missed him, Paw," she said.

"Yeah," he replied, "But at least he let go of Bubba!"

SHAKEY AND THE SHRINK

Shakey said to the psychiatrist, "Doc, every time I get into bed, I think there is somebody under it. You gotta help me!"

"Come to me three times a week for two years and I'll cure your fears," said the shrink. "And I'll only charge you $200 a visit."

"I'll think about it," said Shakey.

Six months later, the doctor met Shakey on the street and asked him why he never came to see him

"For two hundred bucks a visit? A bartender cured me for $10."

"Is that so? How?"

"He told me to cut the legs off the bed."

THE RANCHER

A Texas rancher is vacationing in Australia. He meets a farmer who shows off his wheat field.

"We've got wheat fields twice as big back home," boasts the Texan.

They keep walking and the Aussie shows off his herd of cattle.

"Oh, we have Longhorns that are twice as big," says the braggart.

A little while later, the Texan spots two kangaroos hopping across a field. "What are those?" he asks.

"Ain'tcha got grasshoppers in Texas?" replies the Aussie.

BUBBA SUES

Somewhere in the Deep South, Bubba called an attorney and asked, "Is it true they're suing the cigarette companies for causing people to get cancer?"

"Yes, Bubba, that is true."

"And people are suing fast-food restaurants for making them fat and clogging their arteries with all them burgers and fries... Is that true, Mr. Lawyer?"

"Sure is, Bubba. Why do you ask?"

" 'Cause I was thinkin'... Maybe I can sue Budweiser for all them ugly women I've been wakin' up with.

BEFORE IT STARTS

A man came home from work, sat down in his favorite chair, turned on the TV and said to his wife, "Quick, bring me a beer before it starts."

She looked a little puzzled, but brought him a beer.

When he finished it, he said, "Quick, bring me another beer. It's gonna start."

This time she looked a little angry, but brought him a beer.

When it was gone, he said, "Quick, another beer before it starts."

"That's it!" She blew her top. "You jerk! You waltz in here, flop your fat butt down, don't even say hello to me and then expect me to run around like your slave. Don't you realize that I cook and clean and wash and iron all day long?"

The husband sighed, "Shit! It started!"

WING MEN

Two brothers from Arkansas walk up to the U.S. Air Force recruiting officer and tell him they'd like to join the service.

The officer asks the first twin, "What can you bring to the Air Force?"

"I'm a pilot," he replies.

"You're in," says the officer.

"I can chop wood," offers the other twin.

"Sorry," says the officer, "we don't really need any wood choppers."

"But you hired my brother."

"Sure," says the officer. "He's a pilot."

The brother rolls his eyes and replies, "Yeah, but I have to chop the wood before he can pile it."

A REAL SHOCKER

On business in Mexico, three men get drunk and wake up in jail to learn they will be executed, though none of them can recall what they did to deserve it.

The first man put in the electric chair is asked for his last words.

"I'm from Yale Divinity School and believe in the power of God to intervene on behalf of the innocent."

The switch is thrown, but nothing happens. The jailers figure God wants the man alive and let him go.

The second man is strapped in.

"I'm from Harvard Law School and believe in the power of justice to intervene on behalf of the innocent."

The switch is thrown. Again, nothing happens. The jailers think that the law is on this man's side, so they decide to let him go.

The third man says, "Well, I'm an electrical engineer from MIT, and you're not electrocuting anyone if you don't connect those two loose wires."

SMART SHOPPER

When a woman requested a whole roaster from the butcher, he didn't let on that the bird he presented her with was the last one.

"Do you have one that's a little larger?" she asked.

"Of course," said the butcher. He took the roaster behind the counter, away from view, and made a lot of noise rolling it around in the ice, as if searching for the right chicken. He showed her the bird.

"Better," she said, "but do you have one with a little more meat on it?"

He took the chicken back behind the counter, rolled it in the ice again, and then offered it up a third time.

"Great," the woman said. "I'll take all three."

THE HOMEOWNERS' ASSOCIATION

I have a friend who is president of his homeowners' association down in Washington. They are having a terrible problem with trash on the side of the road that is around his association's homes.

The reason according to my friend Wallace is that being built just next to them are six new homes — big ones! Wallace said the trash is coming from the Mexican work crews at the construction site (McDonald's bags, Burger King trash, etc.).

He has pleaded with the site supervisors and the general contractor to no avail; called the City, County and the police, and got no help.

So guess what some people in his community did?

They organized about 20 folks, named themselves the "Inner Neighborhood Services" to go out at lunchtime and "police" the trash themselves. It is what they did while picking up the trash that is HILARIOUS!

They got some navy blue baseball caps and had the initials "INS" in gold put on the caps. It doesn't take a rocket scientist, however, to understand what they hoped people would think it meant.

Well, the day after their first pickup detail, with them wearing their caps and some carrying cameras, 46 out of 68 construction workers did not show up for work the next morning and haven't come back yet! It has been 10 days since this happened.

Now the general contractor, I understand, is madder than hell, but can't say anything publicly, because he could be busted for hiring illegal aliens.

Wallace and his bunch can't be accused of impersonating INS folks because they have on their homeowner association records the vote to form a new committee within their association, plus they informed the INS about what they were doing in advance, and the INS said, according to Wallace, "Have at it!"

So folks, I think that you could say that Yankee ingenuity triumphs again!

THE PIN AND MRS. JONES

A man goes to the minister at his church. "Reverend," he said, "We have a problem. My wife keeps falling asleep during your sermons. It's very embarrassing, not to mention disrespectful. What can I do?"

"I've noticed this and I have an idea if you're up to the task," says the minister. "Take this hat pin with you. I can see when Mrs. Jones is sleeping, and I will motion to you. When I motion, you give her a good poke in the leg with the hat pin."

The following Sunday, Mrs. Jones dozed off. Noticing this, the preacher put his plan to work.

"And who made the ultimate sacrifice for you?" He said, nodding to Mr. Jones.

"Jesus!" Mrs. Jones cried out as her husband jabbed her leg with the sharp hat pin.

"Yes! You are correct, Mrs. Jones!" came the minister's quick reply.

Mrs. Jones then turned and glared angrily at her husband. Soon, Mrs. Jones again nodded off. The minister noticed.

"Who is your redeemer?" he asked the congregation, motioning toward Mr. Jones.

"My God!" howled Mrs. Jones as she was stuck again with the pin.

"Right again!" bellowed the minister, a slight grin on his face.

Mrs. Jones again gave her husband a real hard threatening glare. Before long though, she again nodded off. This time, however, the minister did not notice.

As he picked up the tempo of his person, he made a few hand gestures that Mr. Jones mistook as signals to sharply poke his wife with the hat pin again.

The minister asked, "And what did Eve say to Adam after she bore him his 99th son?"

Mrs. Jones jumped up and shouted, "You stick that thing in me one more time and I'll break it in half and shove it where the sun don't shine!"

"Amen!" replied all the women in the congregation.

BREAKFAST AT THE WHITE HOUSE

Joe Biden and Barack Obama were having breakfast at the White House. The attractive waitress asks Biden what he would like, and he replies, "I'd like a bowl of oatmeal and some fruit."

"And what can I get for you, Mr. President?"

Obama replies with his trademark wink and slight grin, "How about a quickie this morning?"

"Why, Mr. President!" the waitress exclaims.

"How rude! You're starting to act just like Mr. Clinton, and you've only been in your second term of office for a year!"

As the waitress storms away, Biden leans over to Obama and whispers, "It's pronounced 'quiche.' "

DIVORCE COURT

"Mr. Clark, I have reviewed this case very carefully," the divorce court judge said, "and I've decided to give your wife $775 a week."

"That's very fair, Your Honor," the husband said.

"And every now and then I'll try to send her a few bucks myself."

LOOKS ARE DECEIVING

A doctor examined a woman, took the husband aside, and said, "I don't like the looks of your wife at all."

"Me neither, Doc," says the husband. "But she's a great cook and really good with the kids."

REDNECK CRIME

Two reasons why it's hard to solve a redneck murder:

- All the DNA is the same.

- There are no dental records.

A BLONDE FLYER

A blonde calls Delta Airlines and asks, "Can you tell me how long it'll take to fly from San Francisco to New York City?"

The agent replies, "Just a minute..."

"Thank you," the blonde says, and hangs up.

RELIGIOUS BELIEF

Moe: "My wife got me to believe in religion."

Joe: "Really?"

Moe: "Yeah. Until I married her I didn't believe in hell."

SURGICAL SLIPS

A man is recovering from surgery when a nurse asks him how he is feeling.

"I'm okay, but I didn't like the four-lettered word the doctor used in surgery," he answered.

"What did he say?" asked the nurse.

"OOPS!"

MEXICAN GOLF

Two Mexican detectives were investigating the murder of Juan Gonzalez.

"How was he killed?" asked one detective.

"With a golf gun," the other detective replied.

"A golf gun? What is a golf gun?"

"I don't know. But it sure made a hole in Juan."

CHAPTER 6: OLD GEEZERS

THE PHYSICAL

A 60-year-old man is getting his annual physical.

"Doc, do you think I'll live another 40 years so I can reach 100?"

"That depends," says the doctor. "Do you smoke?"

"No."

"Do you drink?"

"No."

"Do you fool around with loose women?"

"No! Of course not!"

"Well then," says the doctor, "why the hell do you want to live another 40 years?"

DOCTOR'S VISIT

An 86-year-old man walked into a crowded doctor's waiting room. As he approached the desk, the receptionist asked, "Yes, sir, what are you seeing the doctor for today?"

"There's something wrong with my dick," he replied.

The receptionist became irritated and said, "You shouldn't come into a crowded waiting room and say things like that."

"Why not? You asked me what was wrong and I told you," he replied.

The receptionist said, "You've obviously caused some embarrassment in this room full of people. You should have said there is something wrong with your ear or something, and then discussed the problem with the doctor in private."

The man replied, "You shouldn't ask people things in a room full of others, if the answer could embarrass anyone."

The man walked out, waited several minutes, and then re-entered.

The receptionist smiled smugly and asked, "Yes?"

"There's something wrong with my ear," he stated.

The receptionist nodded approvingly and smiles, knowing he had taken her advice. "And what is wrong with your ear, sir?"

"I can't piss out of it," the man replied.

The waiting room erupted in laughter.

STAYING POWER

One Sunday during his sermon, a preacher asked the congregation how many are willing to forgive their enemies.

They all raised their hands except for one elderly lady in the back pew.

The preacher noticed and asked, "Mrs. Jones, why aren't you willing to forgive your enemies?"

"Well, I don't have any," she replied.

"Mrs. Jones, you're 93-years-old and you have no enemies? How is that possible?"

"I simply outlived the bitches."

OLD MAN AND THE PEACOCK

An old man was sitting on a bench at the mall. A teenager walked up to the bench and sat down. He had spiked hair in all different colors: red, green, orange, blue and yellow.

The old man just stared. Every time the teenager looked, the old man was staring.

The teenager finally said sarcastically, "What's the matter old timer, you never done anything wild in your life?"

Without batting an eye, the old man replied, "Got drunk once and had sex with a peacock. I was just wondering if you were my son."

MISSION ACCOMPLISHED

A wife approached her husband wearing the exact sexy little negligee she wore on their wedding night. She looked at him and said, "Honey, do you remember this?"

He looked up at her replied, "Yes, dear, I do. You wore that same negligee the night we were married."

"That's right," she replied. "And do you remember what you said to me that night?"

He nods and said, "Yes, dear, I still remember."

"Well, what was it?"

He responded, "Well, honey, as I remember, I said, 'Ohhhhhhh baby I'm going to suck the life out of those big tits and screw your brains out!' "

She giggled and said, "Yes, that was exactly what you said. Now its 50 years later and I'm in the same negligee that I wore then. What do you have to say tonight?"

Again, he looked up at her, then looked her up and down and said, "Mission accomplished."

DEAD WRONG

A funeral service is being held for a woman who has just passed away. As the pallbearers are carrying out the casket, they accidentally bump into a wall. Hearing a faint moan from inside, the woman's husband opens the casket and finds that his wife is actually alive!

She dies again 10 years later, at which point her husband has to go to another funeral. This time when the pallbearers carry the casket out the door, the husband yells out, "Watch out for that damn wall!"

GO GRANNY

The teenage granddaughter comes downstairs for her date with a see-through blouse on and no bra. Her grandmother just pitched a fit, telling her not to dare go out like that!

The teenager tells her, "Loosen up, Grams. These are modern times. You gotta let your rosebuds show," and out she goes.

The next day the teenager comes downstairs and the grandmother is sitting there with no top on. The teenager wants to die. She explains to her grandmother that she has friends coming over and that it is just not appropriate.

The grandmother says, "Loosen up, sweetie. If you can show off your rosebuds, then I can display my hanging baskets."

THE CORVETTE

A senior citizen in Florida bought a brand new Corvette convertible. He took off down the road, flooring it to 80 mph and enjoying the wind blowing through what little he had left on his head.

"This is great," he thought, as he roared down I-75.

He pushed the pedal to the metal even more. Then he looked in his rearview mirror and saw a highway patrol trooper behind him, blue lights flashing and sirens blaring. "I can get away from him with no problem," thought the man as he tromped it some more, flying down the road at over 100 mph. Then 110 … then 120 mph. Then he thought, "What am I doing? I'm too old for this kind of thing." He pulled over to the side of the road and waited for the trooper to catch up with him.

The trooper pulled in behind the Corvette and walked up to the man. "Sir," he said, looking at his watch. "My shift ends in 30 minutes and today is Friday. If you can give me a reason why you were speeding that I've never heard before, I'll let you go."

The man looked at the trooper and said, "Years ago my wife ran off with a Florida state trooper, and I thought you were bringing her back."

"Have a good day, sir," said the trooper.

THREE EMPTY BEER CANS

Billy and Hillary were married for 40 years. When they first got married Billy said, "I am putting a box under the bed. You must promise never to look in it."

In all their 40 years of marriage, Hillary never looked. However, on the afternoon of their 40th anniversary, curiosity got the better of her and she lifted the lid and peeked inside. In the box were three empty beer cans and $1,879.25 in cash. She closed the box and put it back under the bed. Now that she knew what was in the box, she was doubly curious as to why.

That evening they were out for a special dinner. After dinner Hillary could no longer contain her curiosity and she confessed, saying, "I am so sorry. For all these years I kept my promise and never looked into the box under our bed. However, today the temptation was too much and I gave in. But now I need to know why do you keep the cans in the box?"

Billy thought for a while and said, "I guess after all these years you deserve to know the truth. Whenever I was unfaithful to you, I put an empty beer can in the box under the bed to remind myself not to do it again."

Hillary was shocked, but said, "I am very disappointed and saddened, but I guess after all those years away from home on the road, temptation does happen and I guess that three times is not that bad considering the years." They hugged and made their peace.

A little while later Hillary asked Billy, "Why do you have all that money in the box?"

Billy answered, "Whenever the box filled with empties, I cashed them in."

MEMORY LANE

An elderly couple goes to see a doctor because they're having trouble remembering things. After an exam, the doctor says, "You're fine, but you should write notes to yourself to help your memory."

That night the old man got up to go to the kitchen.

"Will you get me some vanilla ice cream with strawberry?" asks the wife.

"Sure," says the husband.

She asks, "Shouldn't you write it down?"

"I don't have to," he insists. "Vanilla ice cream with strawberries."

Twenty minutes later he returns with a plate of bacon and eggs.

"Damn!" she yells. "You forgot my damn toast!"

THE GEEZER

One day a wealthy 75-year-old man was shopping in an upscale boutique with his young, knockout wife when he ran into an old buddy of his.

Eyeballing the fine, beautiful blonde bending over the counter to try on a necklace, the acquaintance asked him, "How on earth did an old geezer like you land a wife like that?"

The old man whispered back, "It was easy. I told her I was 90."

ONE HAPPY FAMILY

An older father noticed his son's Viagra tablets in the medicine cabinet. "Could I try one?" he asked.

"Sure," his son said. "But make the most of it. Each pill costs 10 bucks."

His dad was shocked by the price. "Don't worry," he promised, "I'll pay you back."

The next morning the son found an envelope under his breakfast plate. Inside was $110.

"Dad," he said, "that pill only cost $10."

"I know," his father said, smiling. "The 10 is from me. The hundred is from your mother."

FAMILY TIES

An elderly man in Pensacola calls his son Bob in Los Angeles and says, "I hate to ruin your day, but your mother and I are getting a divorce. Forty-five years of misery is enough! I'm sick of her, and I'm sick of talking about this, so call your sister in Seattle and tell her." With that he hangs up.

The son frantically calls his sister, who goes nuts upon hearing the news. She calls her father and yells, "You are not getting a divorce! Bob and I will be there tomorrow. Until then, don't do a single thing, do you hear me?"

The father hangs up the phone, turns to his wife and says, "It worked! The kids are coming for a visit, and they're paying their own way!"

GRANDPAS

A small boy was lost at a large shopping mall.

He approached a uniformed policeman and said, "I've lost my grandpa!"

The cop asked, "What's he like?"

The little boy replied, "Canadian Club Whiskey and women with big tits."

GOLDEN YEARS

Two old geezers are sitting in the lounge of their retirement home, complaining about the indignities of growing old.

"My hands shake so badly," says the first guy, "that when I shaved this morning, I cut my face in four places."

"That's nothing," says the second man. "My hands shake so badly that when I took a piss this morning, I came three times!"

NAKED GRANDPA

A man walks up to his house and notices his grandfather sitting on the porch in the rocking chair with nothing on from the waist down.

"Grandpa, what are you doing?" he exclaims. The old man looks off in the distance without answering.

"Grandpa, what are you doing out here with nothing on below your waist?" he asks again.

The old man looks slowly at him and says, "Well, last week I sat out here with no shirt on, and I got a stiff neck. This is your grandma's idea."

RETIREMENT FUN

Working people frequently ask retired people what they do to make their days interesting. For example, the other day I went to town and went to a small shop on High Street. I was only in there for about 5 minutes. When I came out, there was a cop writing out a parking ticket.

I went up to him and said, "Come on, buddy, how about giving a senior citizen a break?"

He ignored me and continued writing the ticket. I called him a Nazi bastard. He glared at me and started writing me another ticket for having worn tires. So I called him a piece of stinking dog shit. He finished the second ticket and put it on the windshield with the first. Then he started writing a third ticket. This went on for about 20 minutes. The more I abused him, the more tickets he wrote.

Personally, I didn't give a shit. I came downtown by bus. I try to have a little fun each day, now that I'm retired. It's important at my age.

WALLY AND ANNA

At 85 years of age, Wally married Anna, a lovely 25-year-old.

Since her new husband is so old, Anna decides that after their wedding she and Wally should have separate bedrooms, because she is concerned that her new but aged husband may overexert himself if they spend the entire night together.

After the wedding festivities, Anna prepares herself for bed and shortly awaits the expected knock on the door. Sure enough the knock comes, and there is Wally, her 85-year-old groom, ready to consummate the marriage.

They make love as one. All goes well. Wally takes leave of his bride, and she prepares to go to sleep.

After a few minutes, Anna hears another knock on her bedroom door, and it's Wally. Again he is ready for more love-making.

Somewhat surprised, Anna consents. When they are done, Wally kisses the bride, bides her a fond night, and leaves.

She is set to go to sleep, but — ah, you guessed it — Wally is back again, rapping on the door, and is as fresh as a 25-year-old, ready for more. And once again, they enjoy each other.

But as Wally gets set to leave again, his young bride says to him, "I am thoroughly impressed that at your age you can perform so well and so often. I have been with guys less than a third your age who were only good once. You are truly a great lover, Wally."

Wally, somewhat embarrassed, turns to Anna and says, "You mean I was here already?"

SENIORS SEX GUIDE

Put on your glasses. Double check that your partner is actually in bed with you.

Set the timer for 10 minutes, in case you doze off in the middle.

Set the mood with lighting. Turn them ALL OFF!

Make sure you put 911 on your speed dial before you begin.

Write partner's name on your hand in case you can't remember.

Keep extra Polygrip close by so your teeth don't end up under the bed.

Have Tylenol ready in case you actually complete the act.

Make all the noise you want. The neighbors are deaf too.

If it works, call everyone you know with the good news.

Don't even think about trying it twice.

THE ELDERLY COUPLE

An elderly couple was celebrating their 60th anniversary. The couple had married as childhood sweethearts and had moved back to their old neighborhood after they retired.

Holding hands, they walked back to their old school. It was not locked, so they entered and found the old desk they'd shared, where Andy carved, "I love you Sally."

On their way back home, a bag of money fell out of an armored car, practically landing on their feet. Sally quickly picked it up, but not sure what to do with it, they took it home.

There, she counted the money — 50 thousand dollars.

Andy said, "We've got to give it back."

Sally said, "Finders keepers." She put the money back in the bag and hid it in their attic.

The next day, two FBI men were canvassing the neighborhood, looking for the money, and knocked on the door.

"Pardon me, but did either of you find a bag that fell out of an armored car yesterday?"

Sally said, "No."

Andy said, "She's lying. She hid it up in the attic."

Sally said, "Don't believe him, he's getting old."

The agents turn to Andy and began to question him. "Tell us the story from the beginning."

Andy said, "Well, when Sally and I were walking home from school yesterday…"

The first FBI guy turns to his partner and says, "We're outta here."

PROOF OF PURCHASE

A little old lady went to the grocery store and put the most expensive cat food in her basket. She then went to the checkout counter where she told the checkout girl, "Nothing but the best for my little kitten."

The girl at the cash register said, "I'm sorry, but we can't sell you cat food without proof that you have a cat. A lot of old people buy cat food to eat, and the management wants proof that you are buying the cat food for your cat."

The little old lady picked up her cat and brought it back to the store. They sold her the cat food.

The next day, the old lady went to the store and bought 12 of the most expensive dog cookies – one for each day of Christmas. The cashier this time demanded proof that she now had a dog, claiming that old people sometimes eat dog food.

Frustrated, she went home, came back and brought in her dog. She was then given the dog cookies.

The next day, she brought in a box with a hole in the lid. The little old lady asked the cashier to stick her finger in the hole.

The cashier said, "No, you might have a snake in there."

The little old lady assured her that there was nothing in the box that would bite her.

So the cashier put her finger into the box and pulled it out and told the little old lady, "That smells like crap."

The little old lady grinned from ear to ear and said, "Now, my dear, can I please buy three rolls of toilet paper?"

RETIRED DEPUTIES

A group of retired deputy sheriffs went to a retreat in the mountains. To save money, they decided to sleep two in a room. But no one wanted to room with Daryl because he snored so badly. They decided it wasn't fair to make one of them stay with him the whole time, so they voted to take turns.

The first deputy slept in Daryl's room and came to breakfast with his hair a mess and his eyes all bloodshot. They said, "Man, what happened to you?"

He said, "Daryl snored so loudly I just sat up and watched him all night."

The next night it was a different deputy's turn. In the morning, same thing — hair all standing up, eyes all bloodshot. They said, "Whoa, bad night? You look awful!"

He said, "Geez, that Daryl shakes the roof. I watched him all night."

The third night was Frank's turn. Frank was a big, burly ex-football player — a man's man. The next morning he came to breakfast bright-eyed and bushy-tailed.

"Good morning," he said.

They couldn't believe it! They said, "Wow! What happened?"

He said, "Well, we got ready for bed. I went and tucked Daryl into bed and kissed him good night. He sat up and watched me all night long."

TWO ENVELOPES

An accountant spends a week at his new office with the accountant he is replacing. On the last day, the departing accountant tells him that he has left two envelopes in the desk drawer and that the envelope No. 1 should be opened if he ever encounters any sort of crisis in the job, and the envelope No. 2 if a further crisis occurs.

Three months down the track there is major drama, all the accounts are wrong — the usual stuff — and the accountant feels very threatened by it all. He remembers the parting words of his predecessor and finds and opens the first envelope. The message inside says, "Blame me!" He does this and gets off the hook. Three months later at his next crisis he opens the second envelope.

The message inside says, "Write two envelopes."

81

DISABILITY CHECK

An old man goes into the Social Security office and fills out an application. Too old to have a birth certificate, he is asked to prove he is old enough. He opens his shirt and shows them the gray hair on his chest and they accept that as proof. He goes home to his wife, shows her the check, and explains to her what has happened.

She replies, "Well, get back down there, pull down your pants, and see if you can get disability!"

THE JOKE IS ON THE DEVIL

There was a little old lady, who every morning stepped out on her front porch, raised her arms to the sky, and shouted: "PRAISE THE LORD!"

One day an atheist moved into the house next door. He became irritated at the little old lady. Every morning he'd step onto his front porch after her and yell: "THERE IS NO GOD!"

Time passed with the two of them carrying on this way every day. One morning, in the middle of the winter, the little old lady stepped onto her front porch and shouted: "PRAISE THE LORD! Please Lord, I have no food and I am starving, provide for me, oh Lord!"

The next morning she stepped onto her front porch and there were two huge bags of groceries sitting there. "PRAISE THE LORD!" she cried out. "HE HAS PROVIDED GROCERIES FOR ME!"

The atheist neighbor jumped out of the hedges and shouted: "THERE IS NO GOD. I BOUGHT THESE GROCERIES!!"

The little old lady threw her arms into the air and shouted: "PRAISE THE LORD! HE HAS PROVIDED ME WITH GROCERIES AND MADE THE DEVIL PAY FOR THEM!"

CHAPTER 7: OUTRAGEOUS HUMOR

NEW MACHINE

A married couple went to the hospital to have their baby delivered.

Upon their arrival, the doctor said he had invented a new machine that would transfer a portion of the mother's labor pain to the baby's father.

He asked if they were willing to try it out.

They were both very much in favor of it.

The doctor set the pain transfer to 10 percent for starters, explaining that even 10 percent was more pain than the father had ever experienced before.

However, as the labor progressed, the husband felt fine and asked the doctor to go ahead and kick it up a notch.

The doctor then adjusted the machine to 20 percent pain transfer. The husband was still feeling fine.

The doctor checked the husband's blood pressure and was amazed at how well he was doing. At this point, they decided to try for 50 percent. The husband continued to feel quite well.

Since the pain transfer was obviously helping out the wife considerably, the husband encouraged the doctor to transfer ALL the pain to him.

The wife delivered a healthy baby boy with virtually no pain. She and her husband were ecstatic.

When they got home, the mailman was dead on the porch.

BUCK NAKED

The weather was very hot and this man wanted desperately to take a dive in a nearby lake. He didn't bring his swimming outfit, but who cared? He was all alone. He undressed and got into the water.

After some delightful minutes of cool swimming, two old ladies walked onto the shore in his direction. He panicked, got out of the water quickly and grabbed a bucket lying in the sand nearby. He held the bucket in front of his private parts and sighed a relief.

The ladies got nearby and looked at him. He felt awkward and wanted to move. Then one of the ladies said, "You know, I have a special gift. I can read minds."

"Impossible," said the man. "You really know what I think?"

"Yes," the lady replied. "Right now I bet you think that the bucket you're holding has a bottom."

SCARY PASSENGER

"Hey buddy," said the taxicab passenger as he tapped the driver on the shoulder.

The driver screamed and lost control of the cab, nearly hitting a bus, jumping the curb and stopping just inches from a huge plate-glass window.

For a moment everything was silent, then the driver said, "Man, you scared the daylights out of me!"

"I'm sorry," said the passenger. "I didn't realize a tap on the shoulder would frighten you so much."

"It's not your fault," the driver replied. "Today is my first day driving a cab. I've been driving a hearse for the last 25 years."

THE PIRATE AND THE SAILOR

The young sailor and the pirate take turns regaling each other with their adventures on the high seas.

The sailor notes that the pirate has a peg leg, a hook, and an eye patch. Curious, he asks, "So, how did you end up with a peg leg?"

The pirate replies, "I was swept overboard, and a shark bit my leg off."

"What about the hook?"

"Boarding an enemy ship," says the pirate. "One of the men cut my hand clean off."

"Incredible," says the sailor. "And how did you get an eye patch?"

"A seagull poop dropping fell in me eye," replies the pirate.

86

"You just lost your eye because of a seagull?"

"Well," says the pirate, "that was me first day with the hook."

THE BUDDY SYSTEM

In Pensacola, a sailor friend told me he was learning to dive in the Gulf of Mexico. The Navy teaches them to use the buddy system because occasionally they dive into shark-infested areas.

"What do you do when you see a shark?" I asked him.

He replied, "Swim faster than my buddy."

SUPERMARKET

A man approaches a beautiful woman in the supermarket.

"I've lost my girlfriend," he tells her. "Can you stand here and talk to me for a few minutes?"

"Sure, but I don't understand how that will help," she replies.

"Well, every time I talk to a woman with tits like yours, my girlfriend appears out of nowhere."

RUBBER CHECK

A man walks into a drugstore and asks the pharmacist for a pack of condoms. Paying for them, he bursts into laughter and walks out of the store.

The next day he comes in again, and once again buys condoms and walks out laughing.

Thinking this is somewhat strange, the pharmacist asks his assistant to follow the man if he comes back.

Sure enough, the man comes in the next day and walks out laughing, carrying his purchase of condoms. This time the assistant goes after him, returning 20 minutes later.

"So, did you follow him?" asks the pharmacist.

"Yup."

"Where did he go?"

"Your house."

SHARK BAIT

Hosting a party in his back yard, a millionaire announces to the crowd that he will give anything he owns to the person who swims the length of his pool. There is just one catch — the pool is filled with sharks.

Splash!!! Into the pool goes a man, swimming furiously. Fins are breaking the water line and jaws are snapping. Just when it looks like the guy is fish food, he climbs out.

"I'm a man of my word," says the millionaire. "And you are the bravest man I've ever met. So what can I give you?"

Glaring into the crowd, the swimmer says, "Let's start with the name of the jerk who pushed me in!"

MY BUSINESS

A 6-foot-5-inch behemoth is sitting in the park cramming his mouth with chocolate bars. After the 12th one, an old man who had been sitting nearby walks over.

"Hello, son," the old man says. "You know that eating chocolate isn't very good for you. It'll give you pimples, rot your teeth, and make you fat as a pig."

The hulking chocolate lover stops chewing for a moment and says, "My grandfather lived to be 102 years old."

"Oh really?" the geriatric replies. "Did he eat 12 chocolate bars every day?"

"No," the big guy says. "He minded his own feedback."

LAST O.J. JOKE

A man is stopped in heavy traffic in Los Angeles and thinks, "Wow, this traffic seems worse than usual. We're not even moving."

Noting a police officer walking down the highway between the cars, the man rolls down his window and says, "Excuse me, officer, what's the holdup?"

"It's O.J. Simpson," says the cop. "He's all depressed. He's lying down in the middle of the highway and threatening to douse himself in gasoline and light himself on fire because he doesn't have $8.5 million dollars for the Goldmans. I'm walking around taking up a collection for him."

The man says, "A collection, huh? How much have you got so far?"

"So far ... 10 gallons."

THE BUM

A bum asks a man for two dollars.

The man asks, "If I give you the money, will you use it buy booze?"

"No," the bum says.

The man asks, "Will you gamble it away?"

Once again, the bum replies, "No."

The man asks, "Then will you come home with me so my wife can see what happens to a man who doesn't drink or gamble?"

EASY MONEY

Joe and Al think there's big money to be made by starting a bungee-jumping business in Mexico. They travel to Mexico City and set up in a square. Soon a crowd assembles. Joe and Al decide to give a demonstration, so Joe jumps. When he bounces back up, Al notices he has a few cuts and scratches. Joe jumps again. On the rebound, he's even more bruised and bloodied, so Al catches him.

"What happened?" he asks. "Was the cord too short?"

"No, it was the crowd," Joe gasps. "What's a piñata?"

DADDY'S LITTLE GIRL

"Hi, honey, this is Daddy. Is your mommy near the phone?"

"No, Daddy. She's upstairs in the bedroom with Uncle Frank."

After a brief pause, Daddy says, "But you don't have an Uncle Frank, honey!"

"Oh, yes, I do, and he's upstairs in the bedroom with Mommy right now."

"Uh, OK then," Daddy says. "Here's what I want you to do. Put down the phone, run upstairs and knock on the bedroom door and shout to Mommy and Uncle Frank that Daddy's car just pulled up outside the house."

"OK Daddy!"

A few minutes later, the little girl comes to the phone. "Well, I did what you said, Daddy."

"And what happened?" he asks.

"Well, Mommy got all scared, jumped out of the bed with no clothes on and ran around screaming, then she tripped over the rug and fell down the stairs and she's not moving anymore."

"Oh, no … and what about Uncle Frank?"

"He jumped out the back window into the swimming pool, but he must have forgotten that last week you took out all the water to clean it, so he hit the bottom of the swimming pool and he's not moving either."

Long pause… then Daddy says, "Swimming pool? Is this 705-5290?"

KILLER CLUB

Walking through the jungle, a hunter found a dead, ferocious-looking rhinoceros with a pygmy standing proudly beside it. Amazed, the hunter asked, "Did you kill that rhino?"

"Why, yes," said the pygmy.

"How could a little fellow like you kill such a beast like that?"

"I killed it with my club!" explained the pygmy.

The astonished hunter exclaimed, "Wow! How big is your club?"

The pygmy replied, "There are about 90 of us."

HEAVY WEIGHT

A young woman was having a physical examination and was very embarrassed because of a weight problem. As she removed her last bit of clothing, she blushed. "I'm so ashamed, doctor," she said. "I guess I let myself go."

The physician was checking her eyes and ears. "Don't feel ashamed, miss. You don't look that bad."

"Do you really think so, doctor?" she asked.

The doctor held a tongue depressor in front of her face and said, "Of course. Now just open your mouth and say, 'Moo.'"

THE FAN CLUB

A handsome young lad went into the hospital for some minor surgery, and the day after the procedure a friend stopped by to see how the guy was doing. His friend was amazed at the number of nurses who entered the room in short intervals with refreshments, offers to fluff his pillows, make the bed, give him back rubs, etc.

"Why all the attention?" the friend asked. "You look fine to me."

"I know!" grinned the patient. "But the nurses kind of formed a little fan club when they all heard that my circumcision required 27 stitches."

PERFECT GENTLEMAN

Charlie marries a virgin. On their wedding night, he's on fire, so he gets naked, jumps into bed, and immediately begins groping her.

"Charles, I expect you to be as mannerly in bed as you are at the dinner table."

So Charlie folds his hands on his lap and says, "Is that better?"

"Much better!" she replies with a smile.

"Okay, then," he says, "Now will you please pass the pussy?"

STRAWBERRY LOVERS

A farmer was driving along the road with a load of fertilizer. A little boy, playing in front of his house, saw him and called, "What've you got in the truck?"

"Fertilizer," the farmer replied.

"What are you going to do with it?" asked the little boy.

"Put it on strawberries," answered the farmer.

"You ought to live here," the little boy advised him. "We put sugar and cream on ours."

PASTA LOVER

A doctor was having an affair with his nurse. Shortly afterward, she told him she was pregnant. Not wanting his wife to know, he gave the nurse a sum of money and asked her to go to Italy and have the baby there.

"But how will I let you know the baby is born?" she asked.

He replied, "Just send me a postcard and write 'spaghetti' on the back. I'll take care of expenses."

Not knowing what else to do, the nurse took the money and flew to Italy.

Six months went by. Then one day the doctor's wife called him at the office and explained, "Dear, you received a very strange postcard in the mail today from Europe, and I don't understand what it means."

The doctor said, "Just wait until I get home and I will explain it to you."

Later that evening, the doctor came home, read the postcard and fell to the floor with a heart attack. Paramedics rushed him to the ER.

The lead medic stayed back to comfort the wife. He asked what trauma had precipitated the cardiac arrest.

So the wife picked up the card and read, "Spaghetti, Spaghetti, Spaghetti, Spaghetti — two with sausage and meatballs, two without."

NOW THEY TELL ME

The doctor said, "Joe, the good news is I can cure your headaches. The bad news is that it will require castration. You have a very rare condition, which causes your testicles to press on your spine, and the pressure creates one hell of a headache. The only way to relieve the pressure is to remove the testicles."

Joe was shocked and depressed. He wondered if he had anything to live for. He couldn't concentrate long enough to answer but decided that he had no choice but to go under the knife.

When he left the hospital he was without a headache for the first time in 20 years, but he felt like he was missing an important part of himself. As he walked down the street, he realized that he felt like a different person. He could make a new beginning and live a new life. He saw a men's clothing store and thought, "That's what I need, a new suit."

He entered the shop and told the salesman, "I'd like a new suit."

The elderly tailor eyed him briefly and said, "Let me see... size 44 long."

Joe laughed, "That's right, how did you know?"

"Been in the business 60 years!" Joe tried on the suit. It fit perfectly.

As Joe admired himself in the mirror, the salesman asked, "How about a new shirt?"

Joe thought for a moment and then said, "Sure."

The salesman eyed Joe and said, "Let's see, 34 sleeve and 16½ neck."

Again Joe was surprised. "That's right! How did you know?"

"Been in the business 60 years!" Joe tried on the shirt, and it fit perfectly.

As Joe adjusted the collar in the mirror, the salesman asked, "How about new shoes?"

Joe was on a roll and said, "Sure."

The salesman eyed Joe's feet and said, "Let's see... 9E."

Joe was astonished. "That's right! How did you know?"

"Been in the business 60 years." Joe tried on the shoes and they fit perfectly.

Joe walked comfortably around the shop and the salesman asked, "How about some new underwear?"

Joe thought for a second and said, "Sure."

The salesman stepped back, eyed Joe's waist and said, "Let's see… size 36."

Joe laughed. "A-ha! I got you! I've worn a size 34 since I was 18 years old."

The salesman shook his head. "You can't wear size 34 underwear. A size 34 would press your testicles up against the base of your spine and give you one hell of a headache!"

PET LOVER

A precious little girl walks into a pet shop and asks in the sweetest little lisp, "Excuthe me mither, do you keep widdle wabbits?"

As the shopkeeper's heart melts, he gets down on his knees so that he's at her level, and asks, "Do you want a widdle white wabby or a thoft and fuwwy bwack wabby or maybe one like that cute widdle bwown wabby over there?"

She, in turn, blushes, rocks on her heels, puts her hands on her knees, leans forward and says in a quiet voice, "I don't fink my pet python weally gives a thit."

JUST MARRIED

A young couple was on their way to Vegas to get married. Before getting there, the girl said to the guy that she had a confession to make. The reason that they had not been too intimate is because she is very flat-chested.

"If you want to cancel the wedding, then I'll understand," she said.

The guy remarked, "I don't mind if you're flat, and sex is not the most important thing in a marriage anyway."

Several miles down the road, the guy turned to the girl and said that he also had a confession to make. The reason that they have not been too intimate is because he is just like a baby below the waist.

The girl remarked, "I don't mind if you're like a baby below the waist, and sex is not the most important thing in a marriage anyway."

And so, the happy couple got married. On their wedding night the girl took off her clothes. True to her word, she was as flat as a washboard. Then the guy took off his clothes. After one glance at his naked body, the girl fainted and fell to the floor.

When she regained consciousness, the guy said, "I told you before we got married, so why the surprise?"

"You told me it was just like a baby."

"It is," he said. "Eight pounds and 21 inches long!"

THINKER'S QUIZ

A female teacher was giving her class of 6-year-olds a quiz. "Behind my back I've got something red, round, and you can eat it. What is it?"

"An apple," replied little Raymond.

"No," she said, "It's a tomato but it shows you're thinking. Okay, I've got something behind my back that greenish colored, round, and you can eat it."

"An apple," replied little Ian.

"No, it's an onion, but it shows you're thinking."

Scruffy little Johnny says, "Teacher I've got something under my desk that's an inch long, white and it has a red end."

"Dirty little boy," said the teacher.

"No, it's a match, but it show's what you're thinking."

A LESSON LEARNED

"Honey," said this husband to his wife, "I invited a friend home for supper."

"What? Are you crazy? The house is a mess, I haven't been shopping, all the dishes are dirty, and I don't feel like cooking a fancy meal!"

"I know all that."

"Then why did you invite a friend over for supper?"

"Because the poor fool's thinking about getting married."

GOOD SPORT

Bruce is driving over the Sydney Harbor Bridge one day when he sees his girlfriend, Sheila, about to throw herself off. Bruce slams on the brakes and yells, "Sheila, honey, what the hell do ya think you're doing?"

Sheila turns around with a tear in her eye and says, "G'day, Bruce. You got me pregnant, and so now I'm gonna kill myself."

Bruce gets a lump in his throat when he hears this he says, "Strewth, Sheila… not only are you a great shag, but you're a real sport too." And he drives off.

LONELY MAN

Paul was ambling through a crowded street fair when he decided to stop and sit at a palm reader's table.

Said the mysterious old woman, "For 15 dollars, I can read your love line and tell you your romantic future."

Paul readily agreed, and the reader took one look at his open palm and said, "I can see that you have no girlfriend."

"That's true," said Paul.

"Oh, my goodness, you are extremely lonely, aren't you?"

"Yes," Paul shamefully admitted. "That's amazing. Can you tell all of this from my love line?"

"Love line? No, from the calluses and blisters on your hand."

A NICE NAME

A guy's talking to a girl in a bar. He asks, "What's your name?"

She says, "Carmen."

He says, "That's a nice name. Who named you, your mother?"

She says, "No, I named myself."

He asks, "Why Carmen?"

She says, "Because I like cars and I like men. What's your name?"

He says, "Beerfuck."

MADE MAIDEN

Two guys were discussing popular family trends on sex, marriage, and values.

Stuart said, "I didn't sleep with my wife before we got married. Did you?"

Leroy replied, "I'm not sure. What was her maiden name?"

LOST SENSE

A little boy went up to his father and asked, "Dad, where did all of my intelligence come from?"

The father replied, "Well, son, you must have got it from your mother, cause I still have mine."

WEDDING CURSE

An old man goes to the wizard to ask him if he can remove a curse he has been living with for 40 years.

The wizard says, "Maybe, but you will have to tell me the exact words that were used to put the curse on you."

The old man says without hesitation, "I now pronounce you man and wife."

SILICONE VALLEY

The science teacher stood in front of the class and said, "Children, if you could have one raw material in the world, what would it be?"

Little Stevie raised his hand and said, "I would want gold, because gold is worth a lot of money and I could buy a Corvette."

The teacher nodded, and then called on Susie.

Little Susie said, "I would want platinum because platinum is worth more than gold and I could buy a Porsche."

Little Johnny stood up and said, "I would want silicone."

The teacher said, "Silicone? Why silicone, Little Johnny?"

"Because my mom has two bags of the stuff and you should see all the sports cars outside our house!"

THE JAILBIRD

A man escaped from a prison where he had been kept for 15 years.

As he runs away, he finds a house and breaks into it, looking for money and guns, but only finds a young couple in bed.

He orders the guy out of bed and ties him up in a chair. While tying the girl up to the bed, he gets on top of her, kisses her on the neck, then gets up and goes to the bathroom.

While he's in there, the husband tells his wife, "Listen, this guy is an escaped prisoner, look at his clothes! He probably spent lots of time in jail, and hasn't seen a woman in years. I saw how he kissed your neck. If he wants sex, don't resist, don't complain, just do what he tells you. Just give him satisfaction. This guy must be dangerous. If he gets angry, he'll kill us. Be strong, honey. I love you."

To which the wife responds, "He was not kissing my neck. He was whispering in my ear. He told me he was gay, thought you were cute, and asked if we kept any Vaseline in the bathroom. Be strong, honey. I love you."

A SIGHT FOR SORE EYES

A man left from work one Friday afternoon. But since it was payday, instead of going home he stayed out the entire weekend partying with the boys and spending his entire paycheck.

When he finally appeared at home Sunday night, he was confronted by his very angry wife and was barraged for nearly two hours with a tirade befitting his actions.

Finally, his wife stopped the nagging and simply asked him, "How would you like it if you didn't see me for two or three days?"

To which he replied, "That would be fine with me."

Monday went by and he didn't see his wife. Tuesday and Wednesday came and went with the same results. Come Thursday, the swelling went down just enough where he could see her a little out of the corner of his left eye.

TERMS OF ENDEARMENT

A man is standing at the register of a hardware store while a clerk rings up his items.

"Excuse me, sir," says a woman in line behind the man. "I couldn't help but notice back in the plumbing supplies aisle that you were calling your wife Crisco. Is that really her name?"

"Oh, no," says the man, "that's just a pet name I use for her in public."

"Really. What do you call her at home?"

"Lard ass."

NUTTY HOURS

A man goes to the post office to apply for a job.

"Have you ever been in the service?" the interviewer asks.

"I was in Vietnam for three years," the man replies. "A mortar round blew my testicles off."

"You're hired," says the interviewer. "The hours are form 8 a.m. to 4 p.m., but come in at 10."

"Why two hours late?" the man asks.

"This is a government job," the interviewer explains. "For the first two hours we stand around scratching our balls."

CHAPTER 8: PARTY FAVORITES

THE ROBBER

Not thinking anyone was home, a burglar enters a home. He searches downstairs, but sees nothing of value. He then goes upstairs and is shocked to find the husband and wife in their bedroom watching TV.

He pulls a gun and points it at the wife and asks, "What's your name?"

"Elizabeth," she replies nervously.

"This is your lucky day. I can't shoot anyone named Elizabeth because that was my dear mother's name." He then points the gun at the husband and asks, "What's your name?"

"My name is Harry, but you can call me Elizabeth."

DOWN THE HATCH

A guy bursts through the doors of a bar and yells, "Bartender, quickly, give me five shots of your finest whiskey and five draft beers. Hurry!"

The bartender starts pouring as fast as he can, and the guy downs it all.

"Hold smoke," says the bartender, "I've never seen anyone drink like that. What's your story?"

The guy wipes his mouth and says, "If you had what I've got you'd drink like that too."

"Oh my God, mister, what do you got?"

"Fifty cents."

FREE MAN

A lady wakes up to find her husband crying. "What's wrong?" she asked.

"Remember when you were 16? When your dad caught us having sex and told me to marry you or do 30 years in jail?"

"Yes," she said, "But that was a long time ago. Why are you crying?"

"Well, I'd be a free man today."

BAD DECISION

A couple had been debating buying a vehicle for weeks. He wanted a truck. She wanted a fast little sports car so she could zip through traffic or around town. He would probably have settled on any beat-up old truck, but everything she seemed to like was way out of their price range.

"Look," she said, "I want something that goes from 0 to 200 in just a few seconds. Nothing else will do. My birthday is coming up so surprise me!"

He did just that. For her birthday, he bought her a new bathroom scale. Nobody has seen or heard from him since.

THE ULTIMATE WOMEN'S JOKE

It has long been contended that there are male jokes and there are female jokes. And there are unisex jokes. Here is a joke I consider a female joke. I offer it to you in the hopes that women will love it and men will pass it along to a woman who will love it.

A woman was sitting at a bar enjoying an after-work cocktail with her girlfriends when an exceptionally tall, handsome, extremely sexy middle-aged man entered the lounge. He was so striking that the woman could not take her eyes off him.

The young-at-heart man noticed her overly attentive stare and, as all men do, walked directly toward her. Before she could offer her apologies for so rudely staring, he leaned over and whispered to her, "I'll do anything, absolutely anything that you want me to do, no matter how kinky, for $20 … on one condition." (There's always a condition!)

Flabbergasted, the woman asked what the condition was.

The man replied, "You have to tell me what you want me to do in just three words." (Controlling huh?)

The woman considered his proposition for a moment, then slowly removed a $20 bill from her purse, which she pressed into the man's hand along with her address. She looked deeply into his eyes, and slowly and meaningfully said, "Clean my house."

YOU GO GIRL!!!!!

DEADLY HABITS

Three desperately ill men met with their doctor one day to discuss their options. One was an alcoholic, one was a chain smoker, and the other was a homosexual. The doctor, addressing all three of them, said, "If any of you indulge in your vices one more time, you will surely die."

The men left the doctor's office, each convinced that he would never again indulge himself in his vice. While walking toward the subway for their return trip to the suburbs, they passed a bar. The alcoholic, hearing the loud music and seeing the lights, could not stop himself. His buddies accompanied him into the bar, where he had a shot of whiskey.

No sooner had he replaced the shot glass on the bar, he fell off his stool, stone cold dead.

His companions, somewhat shaken, left the bar, realizing how seriously they must take the doctor's words. As they walked along, they came upon a cigarette butt lying on the ground, still burning.

The homosexual looked at the chain smoker, and said, "If you bend over to pick that up, we're both dead!"

ROMANCE

Following a whirlwind romance and marriage, reality hits Lisa and Frank. Their sex life diminishes and they began to get on each other's nerves.

After making love one night, Frank throws his pants at Lisa. "Here," he says, "try these on."

She does and looking into the mirror says, "They're much too big."

"That's right," Frank says. "Don't you ever forget who wears the pants in this house!"

Scowling, Lisa reaches down and tosses her panties at Frank. "Try these on," she demands.

Studying the garment, Frank says, "Forget it, I'll never get into these!"

"Until your attitude changes," Lisa replies, "you're absolutely right."

ATTRACTIVE YOUNG GIRL

While enjoying a drink with a friend one night, this guy decides to try his luck with an attractive young girl sitting alone by the bar. To his surprise, she asks him to join her for a drink and eventually asks him if he would like to come back to her place.

The pair jump into a taxi and as soon as they get to her place, they dive onto the bed and spend the night hard at it.

Finally, the guy rolls over, pulls out a cigarette from his jeans and searches for his lighter. Unable to find it, h asks the girl if she has one at hand.

"There might be some matches in the top drawer," she replied.

Opening the drawer of the bedside table, he finds a box of matches sitting neatly on top of a framed picture of another man. Naturally, the guy begins to worry. "Is this your husband?" he inquired nervously.

"No, silly," she replied, snuggling up to him.

"Your boyfriend, then?"

"No, don't worry," she said, nibbling away at his ear.

"Well, who is he then?" demanded the bewildered bloke.

Calmly, the girl takes a match, strikes it across the side of her face and replies, "That would be me before the operation."

HONOR THY BARBIE

Ralph was on his way home from work one night when to his horror he suddenly realized that he'd completely forgotten his daughter's birthday.

He rushed to the nearest toy store and asked the manager on duty, "How much is the Barbie you have in the window?"

"Which one?" the manager replied. "We have Workout Barbie for $19.95, Malibu Barbie for $19.95, Soccer Barbie for $19.95, Cinderella Barbie for $19.95, Retro Barbie is $19.95, and Divorced Barbie is $375.00."

"Hold on," Ralph said. "Why do you charge $375 for Divorced Barbie when all the other Barbies are only $19.95?"

"Well," said the store manager, "Divorced Barbie comes with Ken's car, Ken's house, Ken's boat, Ken's dog, Ken's cat and Ken's furniture."

LOOKING FOR A GIRLFRIEND

When I was 14, I hoped that one day I would have a girlfriend.

When I was 16, I got a girlfriend, but there was no passion. So I decided I needed a passionate girl with a zest for life.

In college I dated a passionate girl, but she was too emotional. Everything was an emergency; she was a drama queen, cried all the time and threatened suicide. So I decided I needed a girl with stability.

When I was 25, I found a very stable girl but she was boring. She was totally predictable and never got excited about anything. Life became so dull that I decided that I needed a girl with some excitement.

When I was 27, I found an exciting girl, but I couldn't keep up with her. She rushed from one thing to another, never settling on anything. She did mad impetuous things and made me miserable as often as happy. She was great fun initially and very energetic, but directionless. So I decided to find a girl with some real ambition.

When I turned 31, I found a smart ambitious girl with her feet planted firmly on the ground, and I married her. She was so ambitious that she divorced me and took everything I owned.

I am now 40 and am looking for a girl with big boobs.

WELL EQUIPPED

Jerry was tired from fishing all morning so he went in for a nap. His wife, Bertha, took the boat out onto the lake and sat in it reading a book.

After about half an hour the sheriff pulled alongside in his motorboat and said, "Ma'am, I'm sorry, but you're in a restricted fishing area."

"But I'm not fishing," Bertha replied. "I'm just reading my book."

"Maybe, but you have all the equipment," said the sheriff. "I'm going to have to write you a ticket."

"Fine," said Bertha, "but I'll be charging you with sexual assault."

"What?" snapped the sheriff. "I haven't even touched you!"

"True," Bertha replied, "But you do have all the equipment."

SOUL MAN

A man is in the hospital recovering from surgery.

"I have good news and bad news," says the surgeon. "The bad news is we accidentally amputated your left leg. Tomorrow we will have to take the right."

"Dammit, Doc," says the man. "What could possibly be the good news?"

"The guy in the next room wants to buy your shoes."

A ROUND FOR EVERYONE

A drunk staggers into a bar and shouts, "A round on me, bartender, and get one for yourself."

The bartender pours everyone a round and they all cheer the drunk.

"That'll be $50," says the barkeep.

"I can't pay that," slurs the drunk. "I don't have any money."

"You son of a bitch!" yells the bartender, who promptly throws the guy out of the bar.

A minute later the drunk staggers back in and shouts, "Another round for everyone on me, bartender!"

"What, no drink for me this time?" quips the barman.

"No way, mister, you get too testy when you drink."

NIGHT MOVES

A drunk goes to the police station to confront a burglar who'd broken into his house the night before. The desk sergeant explains that such a visit is against the rules.

"You'll get your chance in court," he says.

"It isn't that," says the drunk. "I just need to know how the hell he got into the house without waking my wife."

TEMPTING SANTA

A beautiful girl wants to meet Santa Claus so she puts on a robe and stays up late on Christmas Eve.

Santa arrives, climbs down the chimney, and begins filling the socks.

He is about to leave when the girl, who happens to be a gorgeous redhead, says in a sexy voice, "Oh, Santa, please stay. Keep the chill away."

Santa replied, "HO, HO, HO, gotta go. Gotta get the presents to the children, you know."

The girl drops the robe to reveal a sexy bra and panties and says in an even sexier voice, "Oh, Santa, don't run a mile, just stay for a while."

Santa begins to sweat, but replies, "HO, HO, HO, gotta go, gotta go. Gotta get the presents to the children, you know."

The girl takes off her bra and says, "Oh Santa, please ... stay."

Santa wipes his brow, but replies, "HO, HO, HO, gotta go, gotta go. Gotta get the presents to the children, you know."

She loses the panties and says, "Oh Santa ... please ... stay."

Santa, with sweat pouring off his brow says, "HEY, HEY, HEY, gotta stay. Gotta stay! Can't get up the chimney with my pecker this way!!"

MAN OF THE HOUSE

A husband had just finished a book titled, "Man of the House." He stormed into the house and walked right up to his wife.

Pointing a finger in her face, he said, "From now on, I want you to know that I am the man of this house, and my word is the law! I want you to prepare me a gourmet meal tonight, and when I'm finished eating my meal, I expect a sumptuous dessert afterward. Then after dinner, you're going to draw me a bath so I can relax. And when I'm finished with my bath, guess who's going to dress me and comb my hair?"

"The funeral director?" said his wife.

FIVE SURGEONS

Five surgeons are discussing who makes the best patients to operate on.

The first surgeon says, "I like to see accountants on my operating table because when you open them up, everything is numbered."

The second responds, "Yeah, but you should try electricians! Everything inside them is color coded."

The third says, "No, I really think librarians are the best; everything inside them is in alphabetical order."

The fourth chimes in, "You know, I like construction workers. Those guys always understand when you have a few parts left over at the end, and when the job takes longer than you said it would."

But the fifth surgeon shuts them all up when he observes: You're all wrong. Politicians are the easiest to operate on. There's no guts, no heart, no balls, no brains and no spine, and the head and the ass are interchangeable."

DUMB BLONDE?

Two bored casino dealers were waiting at a craps table when a very attractive blonde woman arrived and bet $20,000 on a single roll of the dice.

She said, "I hope you don't mind, but I feel much luckier when I'm completely naked." With that she stripped down, rolled the dice and yelled, "Mama needs new clothes!" Then she hollered, "Yes, yes, I won! I won!" She jumped up and down and hugged each of the dealers. Then she picked up all the money and clothes and quickly departed.

The dealers just stared at each other dumbfounded. Finally, one of them asked, "What did she roll?"

The other answered, "I don't know, I thought you were watching!"

Moral: Not all blondes are dumb, but all men are men.

COP AND THE CON

It's Tuesday. Three in the afternoon. Los Angeles Police pick up a con artist on a Section 872, the Old Fountain of Youth Scam. The con artist is selling bottles filled with a liquid that he claims slows the aging process.

The detective tells his partner, "Frank, check his record. My gut tells me that our boy has played this game before."

Frank reports back. You're right, he's got priors. H was busted for the same thing in 1815, 1887 and 1921."

FIVE SECRETS TO A GREAT RELATIONSHIP

It is important to find a man who works around the house, occasionally cooks and cleans and who has a job.

It is important to find a man who makes you laugh.

It is important to find a man who is dependable, respectful and doesn't lie.

It is important to find a man who is good in bed and who loves to have sex with you.

It is important that these four men never meet.

TEST TUBES

The weekend before their chemistry final, four college friends go on a road trip. They have a great time, but wind up missing the exam by a few hours.

They proceed to tell their professor they got a flat tire on their way back, so he lets them take a make-up test.

The guys study all night and show up on time for the test in the morning.

The professor places them in separate rooms and hands each a test booklet.

The first question is worth five points, and each guy answers it easily. Then they turn to the second question: "For 95 points, which tire?"

CONVICT

Two convicts are working on a chain gang. "I heard the warden's daughter up and married a guy down on Cell Block D," the first con says to the other. "The warden's mighty upset about it too."

"Why?" asked the second prisoner, "because she married a con?"

"No. Because they eloped."

DEAD HEARING AID

An old couple is sitting in church one morning, listening to a sermon, when the wife whispers, "I just let out a silent fart. What should I do?"

The husband whispers back, "Well, for starters, you can put a new battery in your hearing aid."

QUICK THINKING

A grocery store cashier quickly deals with an unruly customer demanding a discount on a damaged carton of eggs.

Later on the manager says to the cashier, "I'm impressed… you really think on your toes. Where are you from?"

"Canada, sir," he said.

"Why'd you leave?"

"They're all just whores and hockey players up there."

"My wife is from Canada!" exclaims the manager.

"What team did she play for?"

BAD NEWS

After giving a man a checkup, the doctor declares that he has bad news and worse news.

"What's the bad news?" asks the man.

"You have cancer," says the doctor.

"Christ. And the worse news?"

"You also have Alzheimer's."

"Well," the patient sighs, "at least I don't have cancer."

WRITTEN COMMUNICATION

A man and his wife were giving each other the silent treatment. After a week of no talking, the man realized that he would need his wife to wake him for an early morning fishing trip.

Not wanting to be the first to break the silence, he wrote on a piece of paper, "Please wake me up at 5 a.m."

The next morning the man rose only to discover it was 9 a.m., and he'd missed the fishing trip. Furious, he was about to go and find his wife when he noticed a piece of paper on his pillow.

It read, "It's 5 a.m. Wake up."

THE GHOST

A young American tourist goes on a guided tour of a creepy old castle in England.

"How did you enjoy it?" the guide asked when it was over.

"It was great," the girl replied, "But I was afraid I was going to see a ghost in some of the dark passageways."

"No need to worry," said the guide. "I've never seen a ghost in all the time that I've been here."

"How long is that?" she asked.

"Oh, about 300 years."

TWO BUDDIES

Two buddies were watching the game when one turned to his friend and said, "You won't believe it. All last night I kept dreaming of a horse and the number five. So I went to the track and put $500 on the fifth horse in the fifth race, and you won't believe what happened."

"Did he win?"

"Nah," the guy said. "He came in fifth."

CHAPTER 9: RIDICULOUS HUMOR

TIRED

For a couple years I've been blaming it on lack of sleep, too much blood pressure from my last job, earwax buildup, poor blood, but now I found out the reason:

I'm tired because I'm overworked.

Here's why:

The population of the USA is about 273 million.

140 million are retired.

That leaves 133 million to do the work.

There are 85 million in school.

Which leaves about 48 million to do the work.

Of this, there are 29 million employed by the federal government.

Leaving 19 million to do the work.

2.8 million are in the armed forces.

Which leaves 16.2 million to do the work.

Take from the total the 14,800,000 people who work for state and city governments.

At that leaves 1.4 million to do the work.

At any given time there are 188,000 people in the hospitals.

Leaving 1,212,000 to do the work.

Now, there are 1,211,998 people in prisons.

That leaves just two people to do all the work.

You and me, and you're just sitting there reading jokes!

ILLEGAL IMMIGRANT'S POEM

I cross ocean, poor and broke, take bus, see employment folk.

Nice man treat me good in there, say I need to see Welfare.

Welfare say, "You come no more, we send cash right to your door."

Welfare checks, they make you wealthy, Medicaid, it keep you healthy!

By and by, I got plenty money, thanks to you American dummy!

Write to friends in motherland, tell them, "Come fast as you can."

They come in turbans and Ford truck, I buy big house with welfare bucks.

They come here, we live together, more welfare checks, it gets better!

Fourteen families, they moving in, but neighbor's patience wearing thin.

Finally, white guy moves away, now I buy his house, and then I say,

"Find more aliens for house to rent." And in the yard I put a tent.

Send for family, they just trash, but they, too, draw the welfare cash!

Everything is very good, and soon we own the neighborhood.

We have hobby it's called breeding, welfare pay for baby feeding.

Kids need dentist? Wife need pill? We get free! We got no bills!

American crazy! He pay all year, to keep welfare running here.

We think America darn good place! Too darn good for the white man race!

If they no like us, they can scram, got lots of room in Pakistan.

I OWE MY MOTHER

My mother taught me TO APPRECIATE A JOB WELL DONE.

"If you're going to kill each other, do it outside. I just finished cleaning."

My mother taught me RELIGION.

"You better pray that will come out of the carpet."

My mother taught me about TIME TRAVEL.

"If you don't straighten up, I'm going to knock you into the middle of next week!"

My mother taught me LOGIC.

"Because I said so, that's why."

My mother taught me MORE LOGIC.

"If you fall out of that swing and break your neck, you're not going to the store with me."

My mother taught me FORESIGHT.

"Make sure you wear clean underwear, in case you're in an accident."

My mother taught me IRONY.

"Keep crying, and I'll give you something to cry about."

My mother taught me about the science of OSMOSIS.

"Shut your mouth and eat your supper."

My mother taught me about CONTORTIONISM.

"Will you look at the dirt on the back of your neck!"

My mother taught me about STAMINA.

"You'll sit there until all that spinach is gone."

My mother taught me about WEATHER.

"This room looks as if a tornado went through it."

My mother taught me about HYPOCRISY.

"If I told you once, I've told you a million times. Don't exaggerate!"

My mother taught me about the CIRCLE OF LIFE.

"I brought you into this world, and I can take you out."

My mother taught me about BEHAVIOR MODIFICATION.

"Stop acting like your father!"

My mother taught me about ENVY.

"There are millions of less fortunate children in this world who don't have wonderful parents like you do."

My mother taught me about ANTICIPATION.

"Just wait until we get home!"

My mother taught me about RECEIVING.

"You are going to get it when you get home!"

My mother taught me MEDICAL SCIENCE.

"If you don't stop crossing your eyes, they are going to get stuck that way."

My mother taught me ESP.

"Put your sweater on; don't you think I know when you are cold?"

My mother taught me HUMOR.

"When that lawn mower cuts off your toes, don't come running to me." (Please, no toe jokes!!!)

My mother taught me HOW TO BECOME AN ADULT.

"If you don't eat your vegetables, you'll never grow up."

My mother taught me GENETICS.

"You're just like your father."

My mother taught me about my roots.

"Shut the door behind you. Do you think you were born in a barn?"

My mother taught me WISDOM.

"When you get to be my age, you'll understand."

And my favorite: My mother taught me about JUSTICE.

"One day you'll have kids, and I hope they turn out just like you."

DIRTIEST COMPANY

Can you imagine working for a company that has a little more than 500 employees and has the following statistics?

* 29 have been accused of spousal abuse

* 7 have been arrested for fraud

* 19 have been accused of writing bad checks

* 117 have directly or indirectly bankrupted at least two businesses

* 3 have done time for assault

* 71 cannot get a credit card due to bad credit

* 14 have been arrested on drug-related charges

* 8 have been arrested for shoplifting

* 21 are currently defendants in lawsuits

* 81 have been arrested for drunk driving in the last year

Can you guess which organization this is?

Give up yet?

It's the 535 members of the United States Congress. The same group of idiots that crank out hundreds of new laws each year designated to keep the rest of us in line.

YOU'RE A REDNECK

You take your dog for a walk and you both use the same tree.

You can entertain yourself for more than 15 minutes with a fly swatter.

You boat has not left the driveway in 15 years.

You burn your yard rather than mow it.

You think "The Nutcracker" is something you do off the high dive.

The Salvation Army declines your furniture.

You offer to give someone the shirt off your back and they don't want it.

You have the local taxidermist on speed dial.

You come back from the dump with more than you took.

You keep a can of Raid on the kitchen table.

Your wife can climb a tree faster than your cat.

Your grandmother has "ammo" on her Christmas list.

You keep flea and tick soap in the shower.

You've been involved in a custody fight over a hunting dog.

You go to the stock car races and don't need a program.

You know how many bales of hay your car will hold.

You have a rag for a gas cap.

Your house doesn't have curtains, but your truck does.

You wonder how service stations keep their restrooms so clean.

You can spit without opening your mouth.

You consider your license plate personalized because your father made it.

Your lifetime goal is to own a fireworks stand.

You have a complete set of salad bowls and they all say Cool Whip on the side

The biggest city you've ever been to is Wal-Mart.

Your working TV sits on top of your non-working TV.

You've been using your ironing board as a buffet table.

A tornado hits your neighborhood and does a $10,000.00 worth of improvement.

You've used a toilet brush to scratch your back.

You missed your 5th-grade graduation because you were on jury duty.

You think fast food is hitting a deer at 65 mph.

10 TRUTHS

Ten truths white, black and Asian people know, but Hispanic people won't admit:

1. Hickies are not attractive.

2. Chicken is food, not a roommate.

3. Jesus is not the name for your son.

4. Your country's flag is not a car decoration.

5. Cars are not meant to touch the ground.

6. "Jump out and run" is not in any insurance policies.

7. Ten people to a car is considered too many.

8. You're in America, you speak our language.

9. Mami and Papi can't possibly be the name of everyone in your family.

10. Letting your children run wildly through the store is not normal.

Ten truths black, Hispanic and Asian people know, but white people wont admit:

1. Elvis is dead.

2. Jesus was not white.

3. Rap music is here to stay.

4. Kissing your pet is not cute or clean.

5. Skinny does not equal sexy.

6. Thomas Jefferson had black children.

7. A 5-year-old child is too big for a stroller.

8. NSync will never hold a candle to the Jackson 5.

9. An occasional spanking helps your child stay in line.

10. Having you children curse you out in public is not normal.

Ten truths white, Hispanic, and Asian people know, but black people won't admit:

1. O.J. did it.

2. Tupac is dead.

3. Teeth should not be decorated.

4. Ranch is a salad dressing, not a side dish.

5. Your pastor doesn't know everything.

6. Jesse Jackson will never be President.

7. Red is not a Kool-Aid flavor, it's a color.

8. Church does not require expensive clothes.

9. Crown Royal bags are meant to be thrown away.

10. Your rims and sound system should not be worth more than your car.

Ten truths white, Hispanic, and black people know, but Asian people won't admit:

1. You can't drive.

2. Disneyland is not the happiest place on earth.

3. The peace sign is outdated.

4. Rice is not a main course.

5. Taking pictures is fun; taking pictures of strangers is just weird.

6. Feet were meant to be grown.

7. You need girls just as much as you need boys.

8. Dogs were meant to be pets, not eaten.

9. You don't need above a 4.0 to graduate.

10. Fanny packs are not an accessory.

PONDERABLES

Can you cry under water?

If money doesn't grow on trees, then why do banks have branches?

Why do you have to "put your two cents in".... but there's only a "penny for your thoughts?" Where's that extra penny going to?

Once you're in Heaven, do you get stuck wearing the clothes you were buried in for eternity?

Why does a round pizza come in a square box?

What disease did cured ham actually have?

How is it that we put a man on the moon before we figured out it would be a good idea to put wheels on luggage?

Why is it that people say they "slept like a baby" when babies wake up like every two hours?

If a deaf person has to go to court, is it still called a hearing?

Why are you IN a movie, but you're ON TV?

Why do people pay to go up tall buildings and then put money in binoculars to look at things on the ground?

How come we choose from just two people for President and fifty for Miss America?

Why do doctors leave the room while you change? They're going to see you naked anyway.

If a 911 operator has a heart attack, whom does he/she call?

Why is "bra" singular and "panties" plural?

Do illiterate people get the full effect of Alphabet soup?

Why do toasters always have a setting that burns the toast to a horrible crisp, which no decent human being would eat?

Why is there a light in the fridge and not in the freezer?

When your photo is taken for your driver's license, why do they tell you to smile? If you are stopped by the police and asked for your license, are you going to be smiling?

If Jimmy cracks corn and no one cares, why is there a stupid song about him?

Can a hearse carrying a corpse drive in the carpool lane?

If the professor on "Gilligan's Island" can make a radio out of a coconut, why can't he fix a hole in a boat?

Why does Goofy stand erect while Pluto remains on all fours? They're both dogs!

What do you call male ballerinas?

Can blind people see their dreams? Do they dream?

If Wyle E. Coyote had enough money to buy all that ACME crap, why didn't he just buy dinner?

If corn oil is made from corn, and vegetable oil is made from vegetables, what is baby oil made from?

If electricity comes from electrons, does morality come from morons?

Is Disney World the only people trap operated by a mouse?

Do the alphabet song and "Twinkle, Twinkle, Little Star" have the same tune?

Why did you just try singing the two songs above?

Why do they call it an asteroid when it's outside the hemisphere, but call it a hemorrhoid when it's in your butt?

Did you ever notice that when you blow in a dog's face, he gets mad at you, but when you take him for a car ride he sticks his head out the window?

ONE-LINERS

Depression is merely anger without enthusiasm.

Drink till she's cute, but stop before the wedding.

Eagles may soar, but weasels don't get sucked into jet engines.

Early bird gets the worm, but the second mouse gets the cheese.

I almost had a psychic girlfriend, but she left before we met.

I drive way too fast to worry about cholesterol.

I intend to live forever — so far, so good.

I love defenseless animals, especially in good gravy.

If Barbie is so popular, why do you have to buy her friends?

If you ain't makin' waves, you ain't kickin' hard enough!

Mental backup in progress — Do Not Disturb!

Mind Like A Steel Trap – Rusty And Illegal In 37 States!

Quantum Mechanics: The dream stuff is made of.

Support bacteria — They're the only culture some people have.

Televangelists: The pro wrestlers of religion.

The only substitute for good manners is fast reflexes.

When everything's coming your way, you're in the wrong lane.

Ambition is a poor excuse for not having enough sense to be lazy.

Give a man a free hand and he'll run it all over you.

If I worked as much as others, I would do as little as they.

Beauty is in the eye of the beer holder.

24 hours in a day, 24 beers in a case. Coincidence?

If everything seems to be going well, you have obviously overlooked something.

Many people quit looking for work when they find a job.

Dancing is a perpendicular expression of a horizontal desire.

When I'm not in my right mind, my left mind gets pretty crowded.

Everyone has a photographic memory. Some don't have film.

Boycott shampoo! Demand the REAL poo!

If you choke a Smurf, what color does it turn?

Who is General Failure and why is he reading my hard disk?

What happens if you get scared half to death twice?

Energizer Bunny arrested, charged with battery.

I poured Spot Remover on my dog, now he's gone.

I used to have an open mind, but my brains kept falling out.

I couldn't repair your brakes, so I made your horn louder.

Shin: a device for finding furniture in the dark.

How do you tell when you've run out of invisible ink?

Join the Army, meet interesting people, and kill them.

Laughing stock: cattle with a sense of humor.

Why do psychics have to ask you for your name?

Wear short sleeves! Support your right to bare arms!

For Sale: Parachute. Only used once, never opened, small stain.

OK, so what's the speed of dark?

Corduroy pillows: They're making headlines!

Black holes are where God divided by zero.

All those who believe in psychokinesis raise my hand.

Excuses are like asses: Everyone's got 'em and they all stink.

I tried sniffing Coke once, but the ice cubes got stuck in my nose.

An apple a day keeps the doctor away... so does having no medical insurance.

I really think the Mars Rover is scouting for the next Wal-Mart superstore site.

Death is life's way of telling you you've been fired.

What we really could use is the separation of Obama and state.

Never play strip poker with a nudist — they have nothing to lose.

If you can't read this, you're illiterate.

It's a small world, but I wouldn't want to paint it.

He who hesitates is boss.

As they say at the Planned Parenthood clinic, better late than never.

UNHITCHED

Q: What do a jack-knifed semi in Ohio, a guy getting a divorce in Alabama, and a tornado in Kansas all have in common?

A: They're all fixing to lose a trailer.

GETTYSBURG UNDRESSED

A man wearing a stovepipe hat, fake beard, and a waistcoat sits down at a bar and orders a drink.

"Going to a party?" the bartender asks.

"Yeah," the man replies, "I'm supposed to go dressed as my love life.

"But you look like Abe Lincoln."

"That's right. My last four scores were seven years ago."

WATCH DOGS

Tiffany adopts two dogs, and she names them Rolex and Timex.

"Where'd you come up with those names?" asked her friend Mandy.

"Helloooo," Tiffany replies. "They're watch dogs."

MIXED EMOTIONS

Q: What's the definition of a mixed emotion?

A: Seeing your mother-in-law back off a cliff in your new car.

SOUTHERN DIFFICULTY

Q: What is particularly long and hard for most southern men?

A: Fifth Grade.

THE SKELETON

A skeleton walks into a bar and says, "Give me a beer and a mop."

SEA KIDS

A number of primary schools were doing a project on the sea. Kids were asked to draw pictures or write about their experiences. Teachers got together to compare the results and put together some of the better ones:

- This is a picture of an octopus. It has eight testicles. (*Kelly, age 6*)

- Some fish are dangerous. Jellyfish can sting. Electric eels can give you a shock. They have to live in caves under the sea where I think they have to plug themselves to chargers. (*Christopher, age 7*)

- Oysters' balls are called pearls. (*James, age 6*)

- If you are surrounded by sea you are an island. If you don't have sea all around you, you are in continent. (*Wayne, age 7*)

- I think sharks are ugly and mean, and have big teeth, just like Emily Richardson. She's not my friend no more. (*Kylie, age 6*)

- A dolphin breathes through an asshole on the top of its head. (*Billy, age 8*)

- My uncle goes out in his boat with pots, and comes back with crabs. (*Millie, age 6*)

- When ships had sails, they used to use the trade winds to cross the ocean. Sometimes, when the wind didn't blow, the sailors would whistle to make the wind come. My brother said they would be better off eating beans. (*William, age 7*)

- I like mermaids. They are beautiful, and I like their shiny tails. How do mermaids get pregnant? (*Helen, age 6*)

- When you go swimming in the sea, it is very cold, and it makes my willy shrink. (*Kevin, age 6*)

BAR-B-Q SEASON

After four long months of cold and winter, we are finally coming up to summer and BBQ season. Therefore, it is important to refresh your memory on the etiquette of this sublime outdoor cooking, as it's the only type of cooking a real man will do, probably because there is an element of danger involved.

When a man volunteers to do the BBQ, the following chain of events are put into motion:

Routine....

1. The woman buys the food.

2. The woman makes the salad, prepares the vegetables, and makes dessert.

3. The woman prepares the meat for cooking, places it on a tray along with the necessary cooking utensils and sauces, and takes it to the man who is lounging beside the grill — beer in hand.

Here comes the important part:

4. THE MAN PLACES THE MEAT ON THE GRILL.

More routine....

5. The woman goes inside to organize the plates and cutlery.

6. The woman comes out to tell the man that the meat is burning. He thanks her and asks if she will bring another beer while he deals with the situation.

Important again:

7. THE MAN TAKES THE MEAT OFF THE GRILL AND HANDS IT TO THE WOMAN.

More routine....

8. The woman prepares the plates, salad, bread, utensils, napkins, sauces and brings them to the table.

9. After eating, the woman clears the table and does the dishes.

And most important of all:

10. Everyone PRAISES the MAN and THANKS HIM for his cooking efforts.

11. The man asks the woman how she enjoyed "her night off." And, upon seeing her annoyed reaction, concludes that there's just no pleasing some women.

PRISON OR WORK

When you think about the differences between work and prison, maybe prison isn't so bad.

In prison ... You spend the majority of your time in an 8x10 cell.

At work ... You spend the majority of your time in a 6x8 cubicle.

In prison ... You get three meals a day.

At work ... You get a break to 1 meal and you have to pay for it.

In prison ... You get time off for good behavior.

At work ... You get rewarded for good behavior with more work.

In prison ... A guard locks and unlocks all the doors for you.

At work ... You must carry around a security card and unlock and open all the doors yourself.

In prison ... You can watch TV and play games.

At work ... You get fired for watching TV and playing games.

In prison ... You get your own toilet.

At work ... You have to share.

In prison ... They allow your family and friends to visit.

At work ... You cannot even speak to your family and friends.

In prison ... All expenses are paid by taxpayers with no work required.

At work ... You get to pay all the expenses to go to work and then they deduct taxes from your salary to pay for prisoners.

In prison ... You spend most of your life looking through bars from inside wanting to get out.

At work ... You spend most of your time wanting to get out and go inside bars.

In prison ... There are Wardens who are often sadistic.

At work ... They are called Supervisors.

In prison ... You have unlimited time to read email jokes.

At work ... You get fired if you get caught.

NOW GET BACK TO WORK!

SOUTHERN TERMS

Artery ... The study of paintings

Bacteria ... Back door to cafeteria

Barium ... What doctors do when patients die

Benign ... What you be, after you be 8

Caesarean section ... A neighborhood in Rome

Cat scan... Searching for kitty

Cauterize ... Made eye contact with her

Colic ... A sheep dog

Coma ... A punctuation mark

D&C ... Where Washington is

Dilate ... To live long

Enema ... Not a friend

Fester ... Quicker than someone else

Fibula ... A small lie

G.I. series ... World Series of military baseball

Hangnail ... What you hang your coat on

Impotent ... Distinguished, well known

Labor pain … Getting hurt at work

Medical staff … A doctor's cane

Morbid … A higher offer

Nitrates … Cheaper than day rates

Node … I knew it

Outpatient … A person who has fainted

Pap smear … A fatherhood test

Pelvis … Second cousin to Elvis

Post-operative … A letter carrier

Recovery room … Place to do upholstery

Rectum … Pretty near killed me

Secretion … Hiding something

Seizure … Roman Empire

Tablet … A small table

Terminal illness … Getting sick at the airport

AIN'T YOUNG WHEN

Signs that you are no longer a kid (or even close):

You're asleep, but others worry that you're dead.

You can live without sex, but not without glasses.

Your back goes out more than you do.

You quit trying to hold your stomach in, no matter who walks in the room.

You buy a compass for the dash of your car.

You are proud of your lawn mower.

Your best friend is dating someone half their age — and isn't breaking any laws.

Your arms are almost too short to read the newspaper.

You sing along with the elevator music.